HAVING
EVERYTHING
RIGHT

Essays of Place

KIM STAFFORD

SASQUATCH BOOKS
SEATTLE

First published in 1986 by Confluence Press.
New paperback edition published in 1997 by Sasquatch Books.

01 00 99 98 97   5 4 3 2 1

Printed in the United States of America.
Distributed in Canada by Raincoast Books Ltd.

Acknowledgments: "Out of This World with Chaucer and the Astronauts" and a shorter version of "Local Character" first appeared in *Sweet Reason,* a publication by the Oregon Committee for the Humanities. A shorter version of "The Separate Hearth" first appeared in *Northwest Magazine.*

Cover and interior design: Karen Schober
Cover photo: ©1996 Nicholas Pavloff/Photonica
Composition: Fay L. Bartels

Library of Congress Cataloging in Publication Data
Stafford, Kim Robert.
        Having everything right : essays of place / Kim R. Stafford.
            p.   cm.
        Includes bibliographical references.
        ISBN 1-57061-097-5
            1. Stafford, Kim Robert—Homes and haunts—Northwest, Pacific.
        2. Northwest, Pacific—Civilization.   I. Title.
        PS3569.T23H38   1997
        814'.54—dc21   96-38097

Sasquatch Books
615 Second Avenue, Suite 260
Seattle, Washington 98104
(206) 467-4300
books@sasquatchbooks.com
http://www.sasquatchbooks.com

Sasquatch Books publishes high-quality adult nonfiction and children's books related to the Northwest (Alaska to San Francisco). For more information about our titles, contact us at the address above, or view our site on the World Wide Web.

For my daughter, Rosemary

Also by Kim Stafford:

ESSAYS
Lochsa Road: A Pilgrim in the West
Entering the Grove (with Gary Braasch)

STORIES
Wind on the Waves (with Ray Atkeson)

POETRY
A Gypsy's History of the World
The Granary
Places & Stories
Apple Bough Soliloquy
Spirit Land (with Gary Nabhan)

CHILDREN'S BOOKS
We Got Here Together

FOLKLORE
*Rendezvous: Stories, Songs & Opinions
        of the Idaho Country*

CONTENTS

INTRODUCTION:
NAMING
THE NORTHWEST

THE KWAKIUTL PEOPLE of the Northwest coast had a habit in their naming. For them, a name was a story. We say "Vancouver," naming an island for a captain; we say "Victoria," naming a village for a queen. For them, a place-name would not be something that is, but something that happens. They called one patch of ocean "Where Salmon Gather." They called one bend in the river "Insufficient Canoe." They called a certain meadow "Blind Women Steaming Clover Roots Become Ducks." They called a point near Knight Inlet "Hollow of the Northwest Wind."

Even as they divided an island into garden plots, the people would not use their own possessive names on the place. One patch they called "Small Round Beach." Another, "Having

Long Cinquefoil Roots." Another, "Having Wind." Another, "Place of Homesickness." When the tide went out, two islands were sometimes joined: "Two Round Things Meeting Now and Then."

When Franz Boas recorded these and other place-names in the last decades of the nineteenth century, the first white settlers were just moving into Kwakiutl territory among the maze of channels and rivers at the north end of Vancouver Island. Reading the book Boas made, *Geographical Names of the Kwakiutl Indians,* it is a shock to follow the active native names along the beach near Alert Bay—"Tree Standing on Flat Beach," "Having Coho Salmon," "Sound of Dripping Water," "Having Brant Geese"—and then to come to the names of the new white tribe: "Cannery," "Court House," "Cemetery," "House of White People."

I want to fight my way back in time, where the new names have not yet pruned away stories with a chainsaw. I want to find new stories, and graft them living to the earth I love. I want to inhabit the Kwakiutl "Place Where Someone Grows Up." I want to camp at the inlet they called "To Decline to Answer." I would survive the place named "Where *Dzō'noq!wa* Cried Out Oh." I would rest by the river pool "Eating Straight Down."

But names on the charts have changed. In coastal sailing guides, directions for crossing shoals to safe water often carry the refrain, "Local knowledge is advised." Local knowledge is that story and place called "Insufficient Canoe." The alternative to local knowledge is shipwreck. There are old ways, and pleasant ways, to avoid this—for the solitary traveler, and for the planet.

If they personified the landscape, the Kwakiutl also naturalized society. The word "kwakiutl" itself is supposed to mean "beach at the north side of the river." A Kwakiutl band took the name of an ancestral creature which had broken out through the ground at a particular place, taken off its animal mask, and become human. For the first two months of life, infants took the names of the places they were born. As they grew, they took many changing names. Adults took the names of wild creatures, and of events in the natural world. We know this from the famous in other tribes: Sitting Bull and Crazy Horse of the Sioux, and Thunder Rolling in the Mountains of the Nez Perce. We know this from the list of players which appeared in a Toronto newspaper for a sporting match of the 1890s:

LACROSSE!

TWELVE CANADIAN GENTLEMEN
VS. TWELVE IROQUOIS INDIANS:

Blue Spotted
Hickory Wood Split
Pick the Feather
Hole in the Sky
Flying Name
The Loon
Deer House
Crossing the River
Outside the Multitude
Scattered Branches
Great Arm
Wild Wind

ON HER MAJESTY'S CRICKET GREEN.

But the adoption of identity from nature did not stop with individual names. The social groups of the Kwakiutl and other original cultures of the north Pacific coast were organized into clans called by such names as Raven, Wolf, Eagle, Frog. A child of the Frog clan walking alone at night might find a real frog's utterance comforting, familial, not only because a frog is a disguised human, but also because people imitate by turns the seasonal lethargy and quickness of frogs. The imported proverb calls this "a two-way street," but that is too thin a way to say it. In native custom and its stories, one life is shared by a mountain named "Elder Brother," a supernatural ancestor named "Made to Have Daylight," a man named "Great Moon," and a killer whale who dances beside grizzly bear in the winter ceremonial. If the Kwakiutl habits of naming were childlike, naive, they were also utterly mature. Their language shows connections where we have made separations.

I want to live in that place by water the Kwakiutl call, in the Boas transcription, *hē'ladē*. They called a meadow at the mouth of the Nimpkish River *hē'ladē*. Another meadow, a few miles east from the confluence of the Adam and Eve Rivers, was also called *hē'ladē*. This name means "Having Everything Right." It is a place where people gather abundant berries and make good life. From that gathering, they gain time at *ts!Ets!ä'qEᵗwas*, "Place of Meeting One Another in Winter," to dance and trade stories. Berries by summer, stories by winter, round and round. "Having Everything Right" is a portable name, an expandable place. It could be what we call Earth. But it will not, unless we sift from our habits the nourishing ways: listening, remembering, telling, weaving a rooted companionship with home ground. I have to *make* my place upriver deserve that name. This is the vocation called "Everything I Do." How can I follow it? Schools trained me to read books, and then to teach subjects. I would rather read the world, and then teach, or tell—but tell what?

When Thomas Jefferson sent Lewis and Clark to read the

West, to cross the primitive half of the continent, he sent with them a word-list he had composed so they might record a sampling of the Indian languages they encountered. But something went wrong. If they did record Indian vocabularies, their notes were lost after they returned east to St. Louis. In the Reuben Gold Thwaites edition of Lewis and Clark's *Original Journals*, we have only Jefferson's list in English. Here is the list's flavor in four passages:

fire	yesterday	a child	to smoke a pipe
water	to-day	father	to love
earth	to-morrow	mother	to hate
air	a day	brother	to strike
wind	a month	sister	to kill
sky	a year	husband	to dance
sun	spring	wife	to jump
moon	summer	son	to fall
star	autumn	daughter	to break
light	winter	the body	to bend
darkness	a man	the head	yes
day	a woman	the hair	no

The list haunts me two ways. First—because Jefferson's list is a thoughtful one—it speaks for elemental life on Earth. It names the essences and relations of creature, time, generation, event. "To kill" and "to dance" are adjacent not by alphabetical coincidence or legal code or logical necessity. They are adjacent because life requires it. "Yesterday/today/tomorrow" is the configuration of both casual conversation and sacred myth. "Yes" and "no" are two sides of one door.

Second—because Jefferson's list is in English only—it

summons the inarticulate, the secret, the old, the lost names for place, custom, and story.

Once, in North Carolina, after an afternoon conversation about Captain John Smith and the colonies, about the Revolutionary War and the Tuscarora Indians all long gone to their tiny reservation in New York state, my kind hostess rattled her glass of iced tea.

"I can't help thinking," she said, "how *we* look upon the Roanoke River every day, and savor our three-hundred-year history. It must be strange to live out West, where history is only a hundred years old, and stories only a hundred years deep." I was chilled by a westerner's homesick knowing: a century is a veil almost thin enough to brush aside.

This book travels for place, custom, and story. As water is pilgrim, I know the urge: to visit all the places I was healed. Water travels as local inhabitant, as essence of tree, of capillary stone, of sunlight pillar in a meadow ablaze with grasshoppers. By that pilgrim's urge, I listen to my family stories, one long generation from the primitive. By that urge, I seek out the speaking places of my own country: Montana battlefield, Oregon fallen barn, North California coastal midden, Idaho eccentric's hut. I listen for the way stories would name our country. This book is the listening. The task of naming I would share with you, for the naming is the active part. I want to learn place, custom, and story for my home. I want to name it in my own tongue, "Having Everything Right."

OUT OF THIS WORLD
WITH CHAUCER
AND THE ASTRONAUTS

*When you overcome the earth
the stars will be yours.*

— BOETHIUS
THE CONSOLATION OF PHILOSOPHY

THE NIGHT Buzz Aldrin and Neil Armstrong landed on the moon, I was lost on some western branch of the German freeway system. I hadn't heard the news in weeks, and it was dark, cold for July, raining hard. With my small collection of words from half a dozen languages, I worked through the lot of a sprawling truckstop, tapping on doors of the big rigs to ask *"Al nord? Dirección Danmark?"* I was getting nowhere, when the Italian driver of a melon truck gave me a smile.

"You American? Eh, beautiful! You see la moon?" He

pointed. The clouds had thinned out. "My radio, it say she belong to you. Apollo. . . . But the Denmark, no. Hey, good luck for you!" I turned to look up at the moon. He pulled the door shut, and I crawled off into a thicket of birches to shiver through the long night in my sleeping bag, spellbound by the moon.

WHAT WILL WE CALL HOME one century from now—a thicket, a nation, the Earth itself? According to a common proverb in the Middle Ages, "Most of us are at home one place on Earth, while experienced travelers are at home many places on Earth. But the truly wise are at home no place on Earth." In that time, people thought life on Earth could only tarnish the soul. The Earth itself was corrupt, and ultimately doomed, along with those too devoted to it. Home was in heaven, and the Earth was only a perilous stopover on the soul's pilgrimage.

This attitude of contempt for the Earth had its own tradition of travel literature (providing the seeds for today's science fiction), in which a human soul casts off the body's husk in sleep or death and flies toward heaven, turning back just in time to see the world, pitifully small and poor as a freckle on the void.

I was lost in Germany, but we are lost on Earth unless we decide what we will call home. We can begin to consider what our home might be like—and to assess what we value as home—by visiting some of these early travel accounts by Cicero, Dante, Chaucer, Milton, and others. In certain ways these imaginative journeys of the past are remarkably similar to the actual travels by astronauts of our own time. We can read the image that came from Cicero's reed pen as a prophetic simulation for

Apollo 11, just as the space programs of the last twenty years may prefigure the human mission in the next century.

Before Copernicus, before Christ, in the first century B.C. when Marcus Tullius Cicero wrote a political tract called *De re publica,* his sense of politics involved both the duties of the individual citizen and the plan of the cosmos. In the final chapter of his book, a character from Roman history named Scipio Africanus the Younger dreams that he has sailed out toward the stars to learn his destiny. It's wonderful out there for Scipio, and like the astronauts of our own time he reports that "the blazing stars" are far brighter than what we see from Earth. As he hovers, amazed among the stars, the spirit-forms of his father and grandfather appear, terrifying him, but then assuring and informing him: he should strive, they say, in the work of the Empire, for nothing is dearer "to that supreme God who rules the whole universe than the establishment of federations bound together by principles of justice." But as he listens, Scipio turns and looks back, and is struck by the size of the distant Earth—"so small that I was ashamed of our Empire which is, so to speak, but a point on its surface."

Cicero was right to be skeptical about the Empire; for all his service to the state, when political enemies seized control they nailed his severed head and right hand to the podium from which he had so often—and so eloquently—addressed the Roman citizens. His "Dream of Scipio" survived, however, as a famous example of cosmology and dream-literature. The ability of this work to look simultaneously inward in dream, backward in history, and outward in cosmology was a model to be copied by medieval writers for centuries. Through the edition and commentary of a fourth-century writer named Macrobius, Scipio's Dream was known intimately by everyone seriously interested in astronomy through the seventeenth century. This included Dante, Chaucer, Milton, Kepler, and others who copied the Dream in their works. Even today, Cicero's way of looking at Earth from outside the atmosphere and yet inside the mind recurs. Though Michael Collins (the third member of the Apollo 11 team) probably never read Cicero, he describes a mental journey toward the stars in words similar to Cicero's: "I can now lift my mind out into space and look back at a midget Earth. I can see it hanging there in the relentless sunlight." The conclusion Collins draws from that perspective also echoes Cicero: "I really believe that if the political leaders of the world could see their planet from a distance of, let's say, 100,000 miles, their outlook could be fundamentally changed. That all-important border would be invisible, that noisy argument suddenly silenced."

The early fourteenth century in Italy was a time of very noisy human argument. That tiny, distant world was what Dante, lifted toward heaven in his *Divine Comedy,* called "the threshing floor that makes us so ferocious," as he glanced back at Earth from the constellation Gemini. Gemini (besides being the name of five American missions into space in 1965) was Dante's astrological birth-sign. He was in exile from his native city of Florence when he wrote about the small, scarred floor of Earth. Like Cicero, he sensed his true home among the stars, and in his vision he did not look back at Earth with longing or regret, but with relief to be away. Earth was a distant chapter in his past.

Another cosmic traveler eager to be away was the hero of Chaucer's courtly romance, *Troilus and Criseyde*. At the close of this story, the Trojan knight and lover Troilus has been killed in battle by Achilles, and his heaven-bound spirit flies up through the eight concentric spheres of the medieval cosmos, brushing aside the four material elements of earth, water, air, and fire, until he bursts out into the realm of the fixed stars and hears the "hevenyssh melodie" that drives the universe. Then he turns and glances back at the Earth:

> And when he was slain in this way
> His light spirit blissfully rose
> Up to the hollowness of the eighth sphere,
> Leaving behind on either side the elements;
> And beyond he saw with utter attention
> The wandering planets, harkening to harmony
> With sounds of heaven's melody.
>
> And down from there he eagerly studied
> This little spot of earth, that by the sea
> Is embraced, and he totally despised
> This wretched world, and held all vanity
> Compared to the sheer happiness
> That is in heaven above.

Especially in my translation, perhaps, this is one of the soberest passages in Chaucer, and some readers have doubted that the author of the *Canterbury Tales* actually wrote it. In a sense, he did not. He only borrowed it from Macrobius, who borrowed it from Cicero, who borrowed it from Lucretius, who borrowed it from Plato, who got it from the Muse. Actually, Chaucer's Troilus is himself quite jolly at this point: "within himself he laughed at the sorrow / Of those who wept so sincerely for his death." Their concerns are so distant, so tiny, blind, absurd. Troilus is jolly at the expense of those he left behind—the wretched Earth and its citizens.

With Milton in the seventeenth century, the traditional language of Cicero's cosmic vision remained, but the attitude toward the value of the Earth began to change. Where Chaucer's Troilus despised "this litel spot of erthe," in *Paradise Lost* the angel Raphael tells Adam,

> . . . this earth a spot, a grain,
> An atom, with the firmament compared . . .
> Though, in comparison of Heav'n, so small,
> Nor glistering, may of solid good contain
> More plenty than the sun that barren shines
> Whose virtue on itself works no effect
> But in the fruitful Earth.

Maybe it was Milton's blindness that brought this change of heart. Maybe it was the chill distances of space that Galileo's telescope and Kepler's mathematics had begun to actualize. Something made Milton and his contemporaries begin to imagine that from out in space the Earth would be small, yes, very small—but somehow winsome, fertile, a garden for a good life. The Earth had been small for Cicero, but therefore worthless. For Milton's Raphael, the tiny atom of Earth holds Eden, and is a kind of heaven in small. From Milton and those who followed him, we inherit both the vision of Earth's smallness and a sense of empathy with it. A hundred years after Milton, cosmic travelers in Voltaire's *Micromegas* first sight the Earth from space: "they discerned a small speck, which was the Earth. Coming from Jupiter, they could not but be moved with compassion at the sight of this miserable spot, upon which, however, they resolved to land."

COSMIC TRAVEL LITERATURE continued from the seventeenth century with an increasing interest in the technology thought to be required for such journeys. Johannes Kepler, best known for his discovery of the elliptical paths and other mathematical principles of planetary motion, wrote a Ciceronean *Dream* in which an Icelandic "dæmon" directs human passengers to the moon. Each must be drugged, protected from cold, assisted with breathing, and bunched like a frightened spider (or human embryo) to survive the trip. (This scientific allegory backfired when it was used as evidence to condemn Kepler's mother as a witch; she was thrown into prison in chains.) Cyrano de Bergerac, on the other hand, imagined a series of flasks filled with dew and strapped onto the traveler's chest; when the sun warms the dew, it evaporates and rises, lifting the traveler away in this bright harness. Jonathan Swift's Gulliver describes the spindled magnet that lifts and guides the airborne island of Laputa, while Jules Verne's first moon-travelers climb inside a gigantic bullet, to be fired from a cannon sunk five hundred feet into the ground near Tampa, Florida. Somehow, all these travelers survive.

Despite technology, Scipio's dream-journey into space still seems to hover in the background for twentieth-century science fiction. For the character named Bedford in *The First Men in the Moon*, by H. G. Wells, take-off is less technological than psychological: "I had expected a violent jerk at starting, a giddy sense of speed. Instead I felt—as if I were disembodied. It was not like the beginning of a journey; it was like the beginning of a dream." Similarly, the religious themes of Dante, Chaucer, and Milton reappear in more recent science fiction works like those co-authored by Larry Niven and Jerry Pournelle (a NASA scientist turned writer): *The Mote in God's Eye* and *Lucifer's Hammer*. Even modern literature set on Earth may take a cosmic view:

> Wait! One more look. Good-by, good-by world. Good-by
> Grover's Corners . . . Mama and Papa. Good-by to clocks
> ticking . . . and sleeping and waking up. Oh, earth, you're too
> wonderful for anybody to realize you.

For contemporary audiences of Thornton Wilder's play *Our Town*, our town is the Earth itself; but this Earth is no longer the shameful speck of Cicero's vision. It is home.

"COLORS STARTLED ME . . . an extraordinary array of vivid hues that were strangely gentle in their play across the receding surface of the world." Gherman Stepanovich Titov so remembers his view of the Earth as he circled it seventeen times in 1961. The early missions went so fast, and were so filled with strict concentration on the flight controls, that the American astronauts and Russian cosmonauts had little time for sustained meditation on the Earth below them—John Glenn seeking out the buttons with the tiny red lights taped to his fingertips, and Yuri Gagarin glancing only at the Earth's "very characteristic and very beautiful blue halo."

When the Apollo program began in 1967, astronauts got far enough from Earth and had enough time in space to really stand in Scipio's shoes. On March 5, 1969, Russell

"Rusty" Schweickart climbed out of the Apollo 9 spacecraft over 100,000 miles from Earth. He was wearing a two-million dollar suit designed—by skill and hope—to protect him from the dangers of space. Unlike the Gemini astronauts, Schweickart had no umbilical oxygen tube leading back to the mother ship, only a simple tether. For this EVA (extra-vehicular activity), he was really outside and alone. As he stood in what they called the "golden slippers"—foot pads painted with pure gold to protect them from the searing rays of the sun—and as he gazed down long and carefully at Earth, he first told his companions inside Apollo, "That's what you call a view from the top of the stairs."

He was Scipio, he was Troilus, he was the angel Raphael. But what Troilus despised as "this litel spot of erthe," Schweickart saw in an utterly different way. "There are no frames and no boundaries," he said later of the Earth. "That little spot you could cover with your thumb—it's everything."

Behind him had been the light-year distant stars, the silent fire of the sun, the moon whirling on its path; yet the soft blue spot of Earth he turned to was everything.

There was a similar moment as the Apollo 11 lunar entry module started its final descent toward the moon. As the altitude of the module began to drop and Neil Armstrong's heartbeat began to rise—from a normal 77 to a high of 156 at touchdown on the Sea of Tranquility—and as the last flurry of technical decisions had to be carried out, as the radio system began, for some reason, to fade at this moment, Buzz Aldrin fired off a sentence to Mission Control that had nothing to do with the potential emergency at hand: "Got the Earth right out our front window."

It was Aldrin who later spent a part of the precious hours on the moon taking bread, wine, and a Bible from his personal preference kit, and celebrating communion. But his sentence in the midst of descent was less religious than it was a simple recognition. There was the Earth. So that's it? Like the copy of Pushkin's poetry that Titov smuggled into his two-week stint in the space-simulation "Deaf Room," a habitual idea like *home* can be tucked away in the survival kit of the mind. A long journey can produce a simple discovery. For James Lovell, commander of the aborted Apollo 13 (which was partially disabled by an explosion on the outward journey, then circled the moon and somehow made it home), it came to this: "We do not realize what we have on Earth until we leave it."

If space-travel helps us to see what we have on Earth by seeing what the cold void lacks, then the astronauts follow Cicero in telling us something crucial about life on Earth. But their message has been read in very different ways. On one side are the advocates of what a third-grader, in a spectacular spelling discovery, once called "the plant earth." Here we have Buckminster Fuller's "Spaceship Earth"; the cover image and philosophy of the *Whole Earth Catalog;* and the contemporary scientists who see Gaia, the Earth, as a single organism maintaining its own life in a way impossible anywhere else. This is home. We must not defile or annihilate this planet, for we are inseparable from it. "It's everything."

On the other side are those who begin with the assumption that we *will* destroy the Earth, and that we must scramble into some kind of exodus very soon. Edward Gilfillan, a scientist once associated with NASA, writes that the Earth should be seen as "merely an overnight campsite along the way; confused, troublesome, unsatisfactory, but unimportant; an untidy place to be abandoned and forgotten." The writer Ray Bradbury told an Italian reporter,

> Homer will die. Michelangelo will die. Galileo, Leonardo, Shakespeare, Einstein will die, all those will die who now are not dead because we are alive, we are thinking of them, we are carrying them within us. And then every single thing, every memory, will hurtle down into the void with us. So let us save them, let us save ourselves. Let us prepare ourselves to escape, to continue life and rebuild our cities on other planets: we shall not be long of this Earth.

The most chilling word here is Bradbury's tiny preposition: "not long *of* this Earth." Bradbury could have said, "not long *on* this Earth," implying that departure would be a movement from this place to another. If we are "not long *of* this Earth," however, our identity is fully independent of it. Ray Bradbury is a careful writer. He knows what he says: the Earth is our campsite only.

And Pope Pius XII told Wernher von Braun (who helped Hitler, and later the United States, to develop rocket technology), "The Lord . . . had no intention of setting a limit to inquiry when He said Ye shall have dominion over the earth. It is all creation which He has entrusted to man and which He has given to the human mind, to penetrate it." According to these views, certain human problems will not be solved on Earth, and the Earth may become the victim of our inability to solve them.

In Jules Verne's *From the Earth to the Moon*, a character

announces that "Humanly speaking, every possible precaution has been taken to bring this rash experiment to a successful termination." Later in the novel, we learn that the scientists did think of everything—*except* how the projectile with three men inside might return to Earth.

"It is all very well to go to the moon, but how to get back again?" says one of the three as they hurtle outward into space.

"The question has no real interest," replies Barbicane, president of the Gun Club which has sponsored the mission. "Later, when we think it advisable to return, we will take counsel together."

So stories go. So our lives go, unless we take counsel together.

We need to take counsel with Cicero before his head is nailed to the rostrum, with Jules and Buzz and Raphael. We must take counsel in many languages. We must speak sternly to our heroes, and listen to our children.

The splashdown of American astronauts far out at sea, their welcoming by a President, a commander, a team of doctors and soldiers to guard their quarantine—all the modern version of Barbicane's Gun Club—is shockingly different from Titov's return. Titov landed on the ground, at the heart of Asia. No one knew where he would come down, and every citizen was out to find him. When Titov's parachute bumped his capsule back to earth and he opened the hatch, a woman ecstatic with blood on her face leaped from her car to kiss him. Driving, she had seen his little ship descending. She had driven into the ditch by the road in her haste to touch him. She ran toward his ship. He lived on Earth again, and she welcomed him.

THREE DAYS after Apollo 11 landed on the moon, I made it to Denmark. It was good to stop in one place a few days; it was a relief not to hitchhike, not to climb into anyone's machine and live at the mercy of their speed. Near the town of Århus, I met a girl named Helle. From her parents' house we took bicycles along the path that wove past flashing streams, dark woods, through meadows thick with sunlight. The grasshoppers still had something to sing about, after so many generations. We were young, foolish, happy. As I drifted ahead around a long curve above the water, she called out, "Wherever heaven is, it must be like this."

I turn to look.

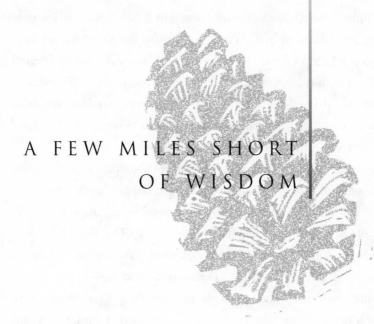

A FEW MILES SHORT
OF WISDOM

A FEW NIGHTS in your life, you know this like the taste of lightning in your teeth: Tomorrow I will be changed. Somehow, in the next passage of light, I will shed reptilian skin and feel the wind's friction again. Sparks will fly. It's a hope for the right kind of fear, the kind that does not turn away.

A few miles short of Wisdom, Montana, I flipped open my sleeping bag at the top of Lost Trail Pass. Starlight prickled my shoulders with cold's tattoo. At midnight there, August meant less than altitude. A long day's winding drive from La Grande had left me numb with the car's buzz, and abrupt dark silence was impossible to believe. But the tall stems of the trees made no sound. My ears were clouded with engine throb and tire whine. The whisper of stars I thought I heard was only a tune my head-bone played. Where I slid into the thin summer bag, I felt a bump of rock dent the small of my back. Sleep blurred my eyes, but I begged the rock to keep me wakeful. Tomorrow, I would drive down a valley that had burned my imagination, a place early trappers called The Big Hole. Tomorrow, Wisdom. The trees' utterance was a pitchy fragrance.

Why did I wish to stay awake? Sometimes stories from thoughtful travelers you trust, or some old book you believe, or the mind's own credulous pilgrim named Imagination will make a place dazzle in anticipation. Tomorrow, The Big Hole. And there was the battlefield that books and travelers and my mind made shine like an icon. Tomorrow, wisdom—if my hunch could be true. Where Joseph and the Nez Perce band were attacked at dawn one year after Custer died, I meant to stand apart from my own life and listen. I meant to stand apart from my century, if I could. The people who raised me would recede, and I would stand apprentice to the place itself. If wisdom could be portable from history, I might read it there in some configuration of the ground. Then sleep.

Midmorning of the next day, I sat faint in the car parked at headquarters for the Big Hole National Battlefield. By the rearview mirror, pine-scattered hills were a blur of heat. Revelation was not going as planned. Dawn had come and gone. On my sleeping bag flung over the back seat, the dew had long dried, and sweat now trickled off my nose. Traveling alone, I had taken the exploratory vow: I will not eat until I learn from this place. I was untaught, and faint.

The personnel at headquarters, the tan-suited rangers inside

their buff museum built to suggest a Nez Perce tipi, had tried
hard to prepare an experience for me. Beyond the glass-cased
photographs and furs, the guns and arrows, they had ushered
me into a little auditorium for my command performance of the
slide show. I had sat alone among the gray folding chairs while
an artist's sketches of the battle flashed before me scene by
scene, and a strident male voice on the tape loop told what
the sound effects were to mean—the pulse of firing guns, a
woman's scream, hoofbeats from invisible horses—while the
watercolor faces of the stern and the doomed went flickering
through their show. Then suddenly the music came up and it
was over. A little motor whirred, and curtains were automati-
cally drawn aside from the windows facing west. There was the
battlefield below, on a flat place by the river. Sun had bleached
the replica lodge-poles gray. One cloud dragged its shadow
toward Canada. On the sill of the view window, two flies had
died side by side.

Now, in the car, leaning back against the hot head-rest, I
understood the chronology, and the battlefield's topography.
From my vantage point at headquarters, I had seen the signs
strung out along the river where named warriors had fallen,
and the pine-thicket knoll where the U.S. Army had been surrounded and pinned down when the tide of battle turned
against them. I saw where they had their all-day chance to
think on Custer's fate, before the Nez Perce slipped away by
night, ending their thirty-six hour siege, abandoning their joy-
less victory for flight. I could follow the events and feel, in my
faint of hunger, a shred of what the original cast of this drama
lived. But where I sat in the car, all this was nothing. The

windshield wore the small debris of shattered yellow bugs.

What did I expect? The past wears an armor that thickens, and I was a fool to think hunger and a wish could pierce it. I had learned the dates and the map, had seen in photographs a long-braided woman and the anguish of old men. I had browsed on books in the National Battlefield gift shop, and I was fed full with history, with news that stays fact:

> During the morning of August 9, 1877, . . . 163 soldiers of the U.S. 7th Infantry and 33 civilian volunteers endured a 36-hour siege as the final scene in the Battle of the Big Hole. The battle began with a dawn attack by the military force upon a camp of 800 Nez Perce men, women and children encamped in 89 tipis on the grassy bank across the river. . . . Follow the trail and explore the military defensive positions. Recreate the struggle of the besieged men and the hostile feelings of the surrounding Nez Perce warriors.

I folded the brochure, and closed my eyes. My government was trying hard to help me. They had made a building and a show. They had scratched out a trail and numbered it, had given me a brochure with matching numbers. I would follow the path. I was grateful. Still my head was a vacant room. Before I took the trail, I had one more try.

Inside, at the headquarters reception area, a ranger with his flat-brim hat on the desk beside him was tallying information from the guest register.

"I bet you get people from all over." I faced him over the glass display case filled with books and souvenirs.

"Excuse me one moment," he said. "1984 to date, out-of-state 87 percent total." His tanned fingers worked the blue ballpoint as if it were a shovel, scooping figures off one page and tossing them neatly onto another. Then he looked up at me. "Yes, from all over the world. Have you had a chance to sign the register?"

"Right here." I pointed to the word "Oregon." The space for my remark was blank, but the column above that blank was filled with "Beautiful display," "Very moving," "Worth the drive," "Howdy from Texas," "My third visit and better than ever." The ranger glanced at me, then turned away to usher a couple wearing identical sunglasses into the small auditorium for the slide show. I could hear the music begin as he closed the door behind them.

"I'm curious," I said. "How many Nez Perce people visit the battlefield?"

The ranger turned to the register, then to his tally. "We had a woman from Iowa last year who said she was one-quarter Nez Perce." He looked into the air between us for a moment, then back at me. There was a pause, and I could hear the muffled pulse of gunfire from the auditorium. My eyes asked the obvious question, and he answered it.

"We know others visit the battlefield itself," he said. "They just don't come here to the Visitor Center to sign the book." He looked into the air again. We both knew this was the part of the show about the Nez Perce warrior named Rainbow—how he was shot as he ran through the dawn mist, how his comrade Five Wounds would have to die the same day by the vow they had shared. We heard the tapered scream of Rainbow's wife, a century distant through the auditorium wall. My eyes asked him again. This time he paused. I had to ask it aloud.

"When do they visit the battlefield?" I looked out the window behind him, as he studied my face.

"They come at night," he said, "and no one sees them." He paused again. "They have their ceremonies in the place, and we respect that." Something brushed my sleeve. He turned. A woman held out four postcards and a dollar bill.

"This has been marvelous, just marvelous. I must tell my daughter. Her children would love this. They're in Chicago, you know. Don't get west very often." The postcards in her hand hovered over a huge open purse, like hawk wings over a nest. Suddenly they plunged inside and her hand escaped just as the purse snapped shut. "But maybe with these pictures I can get them to come. We could drive down from Butte, make a day of it. Wouldn't that be nice?"

"It beats Chicago. I've been to O'Hare," the ranger said.

"O'Hare!" The woman glanced at the ceiling with a smile, crossed herself, spun around, and moved gradually away. The ranger picked up his pen, but I waited. I could tell from the music the slide show was almost over.

"The ceremonies," I said. He held his pen up like an artist's brush. Now the question was in his eyes: how can I trust what I tell you to be safe? Perhaps I have said too much already.

"We don't know much about the ceremonies, just that they happen." We both looked into the air, not at each other. We looked into a box of wind from another time, a box suspended between us, a wind blind to his uniform and my traveling clothes, a box of storm air where the real voices resided and centuries made a number with no meaning. I asked the inevitable question.

"How do you know about the ceremonies? Is there evidence left at the site?"

He looked hard at me, then away. In the auditorium, the little motor whirred to pull curtains aside from the west window. "In certain places," he said, looking toward the auditorium door, "they leave ribbons hanging from the trees." The door opened, and the woman came out before her man. The skin around their eyes was pale. In one smooth motion, they both put on their sunglasses.

ON THE TRAIL to the battle overlook, the sharp-toed print of a doe's hoof was centered on the print of a woman's spike-heeled shoe. The woman came yesterday, the doe at dawn. I stepped aside, leaving that sign in the dust.

But where were the ribbons? Now hunger-vacancy sharpened my sight instead of dulling it. Wind stirred every pine limb with light, green urgency flickering in the heat, flags of color calling every tree a monument. Ribbons? Ceremony? The wind was hilarious and sunlight a blade across my forehead. All along the trail, numbered stakes held cavalry hats of blue-painted wood to mark known positions where soldiers suffered or died. On the high ground above the trail, stakes painted to resemble the tail feathers of eagle marked the known positions of Nez Perce snipers who held the soldiers pinned down all through the afternoon. Feather Feather. Hat Hat Hat. Feather. Tree. Wind. Straw-pale brochure in my hand. Brochure folded into my pocket. Vacancy. Tree. Wind. Ribbon.

Far uphill, at mirage distance, a ribbon shimmered orange from a twig of pine. Off-trail, pine duff sank softly beneath my feet. Trees kept respectfully apart. Earth sucked dry by roots from other pines made them scatter. A gopher had pushed open a hole, and cobweb spangled the smallest dew across it. Then the climb thinned my attention to one small spot of color the wind moved.

Orange plastic ribbon crackled between my fingers—the kind surveyors use to mark boundaries. Not it. Not the wisdom of the place. Not the secret her sunglasses obliterated, not the message that family from Iowa went home without. Not the secret the ranger guarded, then whispered.

A girl's voice spoke from the grove: "The Nez Perce had only ten snipers on the high ground, but the soldiers weren't sure how many were there." She stopped and looked about, then led her parents and sister on along the trail, reading to them from the brochure in her hand. Somehow, she did not stumble, and they padded away through their little flock of dust and disappeared toward the river. A bird's call broke from the willow thicket where they had passed, a watery trill. Patience settled into my mind, like a fossil leaf pressed between centuries. I threaded the trees like a memory. A crow drifted over. A single pine bough stirred, as if the wind were a compact traveler roving before me.

When I found the ribbons they were red and blue. Five strands flickered half a fathom long from a single branch of the pine growing where Five Wounds died. The ribbons knotted at eye level swung new in the breeze, and between my feet a single strand of older ribbon had fallen, bleached white by snow and sun. The age of this custom made me dizzy. The five ribbons on the limb were new as the soft needle-growth sprung from the pine candles. The faded ribbon on the ground lay among sun-bleached needles. The sun-white ribbon on the ground took me back to the hopeful recollections of bead, fur, and photograph cased in glass at the museum, while the five new ribbons conveyed me to the ceremonies of night. I stood so long the sun moved, and a cool shadow rose out of the ground.

Beside my left foot a red ant carried some white crumb by an intricate path: all the long length of a pine needle, careening impossibly over a shattered cone, then up a thin tongue of grass to tumble and rise and struggle on. Following the ant, I saw flecks of blue in its path, and then I was lying down to see tiny blue glass beads strung out along the path of the thread that had held them until it rotted to nothing. So. Before the ribbons marked this place, an older ribbon. Before an older ribbon marked this place, the beads. And before the beads? The ant was skirting around a gray sphere half-sunk into the ground: a round musket ball of lead.

A century collapsed into this moment of ground, where generations of private celebration grew outward from one story. This square yard of pine duff bound a guest register that could never be tallied, only renewed, only inhabited by the night-faithful memory that walked in the form of the people. Twenty steps east from the tree with the ribbons a ton of granite, hewn to a block and polished, was carved with the story as the U.S. Army had lived it through. That was one way to remember 1877: carve the truth in stone and draft a platoon of guardians, write books and print brochures and script slide shows and build a hall to house them all, then carve a trail with numbers like a tattoo on the hill. I was grateful for all that. All that can

make a visitor ready to know. But that public way is not knowing in itself, only a preparation for knowing. Knowing is a
change of heart, physical, slower than the eye's travel across a
page of text, or across a stone dressed with words.

The books, the message on stone, the trail's configuration
would all have to be revised by an act of will; the ribbons
were either renewed or lost by the very nature of their fragility.
Sun and rain destroyed them. Pine budded, and grew. Flowers
withered, and the ribbons.

Suddenly in the heat a kind of fear chilled me—fear about
my fellowship with the sometimes acquisitive tribe of patriots
named America. Even in small things, we wish to map our con-
quest of the planet and the past. My own childhood collections
flickered through my mind: stamps, stones, leaves pressed in a
Bible, insects stilled by cotton soaked with alcohol and pinned
to styrofoam in a box. And arrowheads. Smoky obsidian and
blood-red flint. Modern habit is to lay such things away safe
behind glass, and I had learned that habit well. I knew how to
lift each bead with tweezers, plot and take each bullet up, sift
them all out from the dust and alter them from a part of the
world to an illustration of it. Could I leave the bones of the
story still, and carry only its breath away in my mouth? Or
would I thread five beads on a pine needle souvenir, saying
softly to myself no one would know them gone?

I heard the girl's voice reading along closer through the
grove, as she led her family toward the story of Five Wounds.
His promise to Rainbow, sworn brother, to die the same day
in battle. If one died, the other would die before day ended.
And Rainbow had died. The ribbons were a part of Five

Wounds' promise. He was a hundred years dead and they were new.

From wooden hats staked to the ground I could see where soldiers lay flat to earth in knots of two and three across the slope. The thin grass of pine shade moved, and wind made the trees glisten as sunlight shifted in them, but the hats held still as skulls, each where a soldier lived out his one day's bright terror or luck. But then Five Wounds came sprinting out from the willows into the slot of a shallow ravine, dashing his death-alley straight into the guns of these little hats in crossfire. He knew they had him before the one long breath of his run turned to blood in his mouth, but he lurched to the brow of the ravine to fall at my feet beneath these ribbons, beneath the bullets scattered later by night to heal his name, and now beneath the low voice of this girl practicing the ceremony of literate culture with a paper in her hands:

"Five Wounds charged up the gulch and was killed without a doubt. . . ."

"What are the ribbons for?" her little sister asked, interrupting. Leaning on each other, the parents stepped back, gentled by fatigue. The girl stopped reading and looked up.

"What ribbons?" Her eyes squinted for distance, then focused on the paper again. "It doesn't say."

DRIVING ON, I was tipsy with gratitude. Fenceposts passing fast out the open window were pine with the bark left on, and they chirred like insects—whisp, whisp, whisp, whisp—down the long straight road heat blurred. The mountains stood up in a blue ring distant around the valley. Sage entered me, then a hint of cut hay, then the wind-twisted fragrance of smoke and manure from a little clutter of ranch buildings at the long, tapered end of its drive. After a few miles, Wisdom itself was a truck filled with horses saddled and stamping fitfully, a wall of deer antlers below a TV satellite dish, country music aching from loudspeakers nailed to the trading post façade, and a poster at the bar advertising a rodeo memorial for two teenagers killed in a car wreck: "Only working cowboys within a hundred-mile radius of Wisdom will be eligible for the purse."

Then Wisdom was behind, and I was sailing out the highway banked on the long curves the river led east, past fields where ponies put their ears forward to the passing snap of my fingers in the wind, and on into the open country that somehow forgot to get changed from plain gray sage and rocky bluffs, from ravines dark with willow shade and stone litter glittering down a hillside where hard rain scattered it, and the trees getting scarce for the long dry of days like this.

I was changed. The ribbons had pulled the sky right down to the ground, and tethered my soul to a story. If I was not changed, not wise, I had a way to become so. I possessed a vision-book of one moment, a story small as the pitchy pith of juniper seed to nibble for the rest of my life.

Then I saw the bear, and stopped the car. It was a young bear, about my size and black as lightning's footprint, rambling northeast along the south-facing slope of the river gully, in the direction the Nez Perce survivors of the battle had taken toward Canada, toward the place called Bear Paws where they were finally stopped. When I climbed out and the car door made a sound, the bear didn't shy suddenly off to the side like I've seen bear do, or coyotes feeling the bullet-blast of human sight graze their shoulders. Wind riffled the bear's fur, and it turned slowly to look over its shoulder from about a hundred yards off. Even at that distance, I could see the close squint of eyes, the nostril-flare of pertinent curiosity. She lifted her nose to know me by the thin ribbon of scent wind trailed out. Not in haste but not wasting daylight, she turned away, head swung down, and she ambled away over the open slope of sage, climbing toward the bluffs at the crest of my sight.

The afternoon still: a wisp of wind-whistle in sage, and the little rattle of stone where the bear's paws swung along. I felt history receding with the click and scatter of her steps, as if I saw the last run of a river trail away down the geologic trough of its bed. What made seeing not enough? What made me want to meet that shaggy woman, not merely see her sip the wind over her shoulder and turn away?

In the car I stared at the choke, the odometer, the radio. The paltry pleasures of speed and distance were mine. How had exhilaration evaporated so fast? The dwindling hummock of the bear was approaching the ridge as I turned the key and swung out, cruised a half mile out of sight around the bend, killed the engine and coasted to a stop, left the white car's pod, the road's gray vine, and climbed on foot toward the ridge. A need for quiet now—now that the bear's scent would follow the wind toward me as her path met mine. She would not know I was there. Now she would come close enough with her poor eyes to see my shape rise up.

At the brow of the ridge, along her natural way, I crouched breathless among sage scrub abuzz with insect tremor and sound. The ground fell away to my left toward the river's long curve. To my right stretched miles of open sage. The only hidden ground lay before me, toward the afternoon sun. There, I had seen the bear aim straight this way. There was no alternative for her but to come up over the hump of ground to meet me. If she turned, I would see her on the open ground to either side. From here, I would see first the black hackles of her back like a ruffled wave over the sage horizon, then the bobbing rims of her ears, then her small, close-set eyes, her lips pulled back to pant—and then I would stand up slowly.

My fear brightened the hillside as with sweat. Every tongue of sage leaf glittered, and the sand before me was exact with sunlight. I faced west, where the breeze at my face trembled cool with rumor and scent: the smoky scent of bruised stone, the thin sweet fragrance of crushed grass. Soon, it would be bear. Soon my heart would stop its percussive haste. I would stand, and speak. Some compliment. Some respectful word.

Wind rattled the dry sticks of the sage. My bones held an old juniper's arthritic stance. The sun moved, and an ant came toward me, crossed a fathom of epic sand, and disappeared into the shade I cast. Blank wind chilled my face. Somehow, the bear slipped past my vision by some private tunnel of her own power.

The risk I took to meet the bear was a responsibility greater than being husband, father, or son. But it was not enough. I was no true citizen of wisdom, but spent all I had on being afraid. So busy with fear, I had not enough hospitality for danger and change. There was only dwindling light on the place itself.

I stood up dizzy with regret, stumbled back to the car, slid in the key, drove on, drove two hundred miles east by a path of dash-lined curves, of skid marks and guard rails dented with rust, of gas-stop exits numbered monotonous, of passing and being passed by wind-tailed trucks made brazen by their size, drove miles of signs promising greater distances to Bozeman than Butte, to Billings than Bozeman, and miles of travel without change. And Change was my sworn brother—that we would die the same day, as Five Wounds swore to Rainbow, and fulfilled.

The day ended in Billings, where the librarians were meeting. They had come by air and car from Missoula, Boise, Seattle, Portland. They talked about change, and tradition. After the banquet, I stood at the podium, the microphone one breath's distance from my lips, and spoke: The Role of the Humanist in a Technological Age. I was not able to tell what I was learning, only what I had learned—too long before to be true. There was kind applause, and draining of the last wine. At the end, at midnight in the twenty-third floor conference suite, among the swirl of my smart companions, good people of my tribe holding their drinks in clear cups that tingled with the buzz and din of talk—at the end I saw the crowd divide when lightning began to play over the city below us. Some drew back against the wall. "Should we really be up here? Is the basement safer now? The stairwell . . . ?"

But some set down their champagne cups to press outward against tall windows, as lightning came faster toward us over the grid of streets, the jagged light that started fires that night all over Montana. I stepped toward the bright hot ribbons hanging down, and the din of our talk was hushed. One light on every thing: antenna, automobile, hilarious newspaper debris rolling through the streets below, the dark distant hills. In a flash our party's reflection in the window eclipsed—the ribbons hanging down, and a girl's voice telling the story, the burnt ozone scent of change come through sage to meet me.

STILL, I am afraid. A man of my own tribe trusted me with the story of the ribbons, and I trust you with the beads. He may have been wrong, and I may be wrong. I would let the place alone, but it will not let me alone.

They say in Japan stands a building filled with national cultural treasures so valuable no steel door, no lock is strong enough to protect them from thieves. Instead of such a door, the state has hired an old man to watch the building in case of fire. He slowly walks about the building, then rests in the shade. Tied by thread to the simple door-latch, a note from the Emperor explains the supreme value of the treasury inside. There is no other lock.

I would make such a note for a square yard of ground in Montana, a few miles west of Wisdom.

THE STORY
THAT SAVED LIFE

MEMORY IS MADE as a quilt is made. From the whole cloth of time, frayed scraps of sensation are pulled apart, and then pieced back together in a pattern with a name: Grandmother's Garden, Drunkard's Path to Dublin, Double Wedding Ring. Call this, The Story That Saved Life.

On the way into Wallowa County in northeastern Oregon, just at the edge of the quilt, the hem of the story, you come over a rise. The wheat and hayloft blocks of the farms look about the same, the hill-patch pines and long seam of the road dashing on into a swale. But there are signs. One sign warns that no potatoes, hay, or wheat are to be carried into the County. The place is disease-free. The ground is pure. Take a deep breath, and listen.

THERE IS A TOWN called Elgin. They say one night the door of the doctor's office jangled open. There was a woman full in her form, expecting. Behind her stood a thin rail of husband with a hard glint to his eye.

"Good evening. What can I do for you?" The doctor rose up from the rocking chair.

"We're ready for the baby." The husband stepped around his woman. He wasn't from town. Mud stiffened his pants to the knees.

The doctor turned to the woman. "How long have you been in labor?"

"I'm not." She bobbed and rolled before him, trying to curtsy. "Not yet, sir."

"But we're ready for the baby." The husband moved behind her and nudged her forward, his boots nipping her heels.

The doctor stepped back. He should have turned on more light, but it had been almost time to close. The woman was a dim silhouette against the evening snowlight of the window.

"If you're not in labor yet, there's not much I can do. Can you stay with friends in town?" The doctor looked at her. Then from behind the woman a knife glittered in the husband's hand.

"I said we're ready, now." The husband came around his woman again and faced the doctor, the canopy of light from the desk lamp coming up only as far as his hand and its hunting knife. There was grease under his fingernails. "I got to leave for a while—elk season. Don't want none of this happening while I'm gone." The woman whispered a long breath.

"Okay," said the doctor. "If it's that way, let me get my bag." Staying in the pool of light, he turned and snapped open the black case on the table beside. His hand went inside. When it came out, there was a pistol—not exactly aimed anywhere, but part of his gesture.

"You folks are just going to have to wait. Now go on home, or somewhere. Let me know when it's really time. I'll be glad to help you then."

OLD JOSEPH was born before anyone wanted to raise hay in the Wallowa Valley. When the first whites came, Old Joseph planted a row of poles along the divide where the signs about pure seed potatoes now stand. The poles were not a fence, but a mark of understanding. But only the Nez Perce understood what that boundary meant.

After the Nez Perce were driven away, Old Joseph's grave at Wallowa Forks happened to coincide with a gravel quarry. The Indians came back, loaded his bones in a buckboard, and carried them south to Wallowa Lake. A bronze plaque there tells about it. At the lake is a mound of stone. At the Forks, where the bands used to gather, there is only the damp pit of the quarry.

PAST ELGIN, along the Minam Canyon rim is a place where people scan the far slope for elk. Some do strange things in elk season. Some do strange things all the time. The mountains let you be that way. Beyond the Minam Canyon into the canyon of the Wallowa, every curve in the river road has a story, and every straight run is the pause before a story. Story, story, story, the map-quilt gets made, gets folded for the pocket of the mind: that house with the three little cabins strung out behind, where the Civil War colonel, fled from Louisiana to Oregon, planted his slaves. Story. That road out Bear Creek where a logger stole a cement highway bridge from the U.S. government, loaded it on his truck somehow, and disappeared. Story. That single grave of the Indian girl. Story. School children heard the story and built her grave a picket fence, painted it white. In the bluff over town a cave is carved with children's names. Dusk erased them. The cave is a stone telescope, and Wallowa glimmers far away. Measure that distance in years.

HOW MANY GENERATIONS to work a story down to size, to rub away the burrs and sawdust of its making? You have to forget 90 percent of what happens if you want to tell the story right. So said Wilma, substitute teacher in residence at Wallowa School. She was a teacher by story, story alone. Something about the way her dress, softened by a lifetime of washings, hung down. Something about the spark her eyes kindled. Something about her hands held up to shape a face that's been long buried but burns in the air:

"My uncles, they all had handsome faces, but Earl was the darling—dark hair, chin like a pretty little axe, but he could talk blue. Those eyes. Had to leave West Virginia in a big hurry. We never did know why. But he made the best white lightning you ever dreamed. Kept a Mason jar full in the refrigerator. Liked his cold.

"Well, he comes home pretty looped one night, along in the spring, shouting about the cabbage maggots. We hear him slam the car door and shout, 'Damn you, maggots! I'll fix you!'

"We hear him fumbling around in the hall, stumbling

around. I remember I figured he was just trying to make it to his bedroom. But no. I hear the snap of his shotgun action getting loaded.

" 'You think just because you're little, you're safe!' That line wakes everybody up. I can hear Mama call out, 'Earl! I want you calm!' But then he starts for the back door, and I sit up in bed. It's just starting to get light. I pull the curtains back when I hear the screen door bang shut and the dogs whimper as they get out of Earl's way.

" 'Your time's come, so stand up all of you and take it!'

" 'Earl!' Mama's in the hall, but I can see she's too late. Earl's in the garden, raising the shotgun toward the east. And just as the sun's first rays flicker onto his face, he fires off both barrels level over the garden into the trees out east.

"BOOM! BARRROOOOM! He has a wild, satisfied grin on his face, and all of Mama's calling from the back porch can't make it go away.

"You know, we never did have trouble with the cabbage maggots after that. I know it sounds crazy. It is crazy. Gardening is like that. And Earl's white lightning makes things like that too. We took it for a saying in the family, whenever things got so impossible we didn't have any logical thing to do, we'd say, 'Fire two shots toward the rising sun!' And after we said that, and thought about Earl standing there so happy his pants were about to fall down, nothing seemed quite so bad."

BEFORE I CAME to Wallowa County, I was warned by a city friend: "You've got to watch it out there. That's real gun country, you know. Did you read once there were these two Wallowa brothers bagged elk out of season, and when this cop went out to arrest them, they shot him? They had to call out the National Guard and surround the place. Sure enough, through binoculars they could see that cop car shot full of holes and dragged into the barn. Had a big shoot-out, before they finally nailed those two guys. That's still the real West out there. You better watch it!"

When I had been in Wallowa for a few weeks, I asked a friend, "What's this about the two brothers who did some poaching, then shot the cop, and the National Guard surrounded their place and shot them down?"

"Oh, sure. It's true, except it didn't happen quite like that. You see, there were these two brothers who had some ground in wheat, and the elk got to grazing in there every day, just like it was their own private pasture. Brothers figured since they'd fattened that whole elk herd, they had the right to slaughter one, just like it was their own stock. So they bagged one and hung it up in the barn.

"Well, these two cops drove out there to arrest them, but it was kind of a joke. *Everybody* poaches. But the two cops go out to give them a warning or something, anyway, and one of the brothers gets so upset he hooks a chain to the rear axle on the cop car, drags it into the barn, locks the door, and the cops can't do a thing but walk back to town.

"There wasn't any shooting, though. This is the West, but it's not *that* wild."

When I had been in Wallowa several months, I asked an old-timer, "What's this about the two brothers who did some poaching just like everybody does, but then they dragged a cop car into their barn with a tractor and locked the door, and the cops had to walk back to town?"

"Where'd you hear that? It's true, all except the part about the barn. There are these two brothers up on Alder Slope. They've got a nice little piece of wheat ground up there against the mountains, you know. Up where the elk will get you if the cold snap don't. It ain't hardly poaching. It's more like taking a cut off your own herd. But say, that reminds me about this hunter one time came out here from Portland—brand new squeaky hunting clothes he got out of some catalogue, some fancy spit and polish boots, and a new gun that didn't hardly have the sale tag cleaned off it.

"Well, this Portland hunter stops in at the market—you know that little market in Enterprise, on the left just before you head out toward Joseph? He stops in there to buy a little beer, and the clerk boy starts in admiring his outfit:

" 'Mister, you look like you're about to get yourself an elk.'

" 'I sure hope so,' says this Portland hunter. But then he lowers his voice and says, 'Only trouble is, I've never seen one.'

" 'Golly, mister!' The clerk boy looks around, and then leans forward with his hands on the cash register. 'I'm really glad you mentioned that, mister, because there could be some real problems if you made a mistake.'

" 'Anything you could tell me,' says this Portland hunter. 'I'd really appreciate it.' A line is forming up behind the hunter, and the boy has to lower his voice even more.

" 'Well, here goes. You drive on out of town, you'll start to see herds of these elk in the pastures beside the road. They have big red and white patches on their sides, little bitty short horns that curve up like this by their ears, and when you stop your rig, they'll all turn around and look at you. That's a pretty good time to get off a shot.'

" 'Hey, thanks for the tip,' says this hunter, wanting to shake the boy's hand. 'I really appreciate it.'

"So the hunter goes out, but the next morning he comes back in all excited, says to the boy still standing there at the cash register, 'I got my elk, thanks to you! Want to see it?'

" 'Sure,' says the kid, jamming his dusting feathers into his back pocket. He gestures toward some men to leave their shopping carts and follow along.

" 'I got him right out here in the pickup—nice rack on him, too.' The hunter leads them all out to the parking lot, where the kid looks over the side of the long box on that shiny new truck. Sure enough, there's a nice big steer lying there shot all to hell. And the kid's about ready to bust out laughing, when he notices his own daddy's brand burned into the hide.

"Yeah, the kid never bragged on that story too much, but everybody else sure loves to tell it."

"The hunter got the steer, but you got the story."

"Yeah, that's right. So these two brothers, they had their elk strung up in the barn when the cop car drives up. Those two cops did a little poaching on the side themselves. You have to, with the economy what it is. They'd just come out to razz their friends a little, you know. Well, these two cops start reading them the statute about poaching, while the four of them have some beer, and them all laughing about it, and one of the brothers gets to horsing around on the tractor. Had the forklift rigged on the back, I guess. And he kind of accidentally pokes a hole in the radiator on the cop car. Just a little hole that looked like nothing. Didn't even hurt the grille.

"But the two cops, by the time they'd finished their beers and got halfway back to town, their radiator was dry. They had to hitchhike the rest of the way."

I WAS TO VISIT the school at Joseph, and I would tell a story to the high school class. It was a strange thing to carry *Coyote Was Going There*, a book of Nez Perce tales, into Wallowa County, the home country of the Nez Perce, but where the latest census shows not one Nez Perce woman, man, or child. From my second-story apartment window, I looked up from the book at the hills: three trees huddled together on the horizon. A hundred years ago, the Nez Perce all were driven out. A twist of pride and guilt hangs in the air. Chief Joseph's image tops the masthead of the weekly *Chieftain*, but Nez Perce people only come for the rodeo. And lately, they've asked for money to come to that, to wear their costumes and ride in the parade. Then they go back to their exile at Lapwai or Colville.

It was a strange thing to leave my book of tales, and carry one of its stories in my head to the town called Joseph, to walk into an all-white class and unfold a narrative rooted to the place we stole. I decided to try a Nez Perce tale that had made me laugh when I read it silently to myself. Coyote is such a fool. He postures and hopes, makes all the predictable mistakes, then sits alone on a hill waiting for the world to change, waiting to see his foolish wish come true and the world forgive him. In my apartment I had laughed, and put the book down. Now I stood in front of the class. I could not remember the story just as it was, word for word, but it would have been too strange to read it, so I told this:

COYOTE HAD A WIFE, and his wife died, and he mourned her for a time. But then a shadow came to speak with him.

"Coyote, if you do just as I tell you, your life will be as it was. Your wife will live with you as before."

"Tell me, and I will do as you say."

"Follow me five days," said the shadow, "and do as I do. Then you will see your wife. You may bring her back among the living, if you do right."

They had been traveling most of one day, when the shadow said, "Look what fine horses are running there."

Coyote saw nothing, but he held his hand up over his eyes, nodding as the shadow did.

"Look what fine horses are running there," Coyote said. And they traveled.

One day, the shadow said, "Let us bend down these branches and gather serviceberries for our meal." The shadow pulled at the air where nothing grew, and chewed.

"Let us bend down these branches and gather service-berries for our meal," said Coyote, and he scooped the air with his hands and chewed.

The fifth day, they came to a low hill.

"Soon it will be dark," the shadow said. "Then we can enter the lodge of the dead. You will see your wife." Coyote and the shadow sat down to wait. The sun moved not at all, then slowly, then it went down. The shadow stood up.

"It is time to go inside." The shadow's hands seemed to be lifting a door-flap. The shadow bent down and went through.

"It is time to go inside," said Coyote. He raised his hands, bent down, stepped forward. People were singing. They were gathered about a fire. Farther along was another fire, then another. Coyote walked from one fire to another, searching the faces of the dead. There was his wife.

The shadow said, "As you walk with her toward your home, you must not touch her. Remember that one thing."

The sun came up. The fires were gone, and the people, the lodge, and the shadow. Beside Coyote was something in the air. She followed him all day. That night, beside their fire, Coyote looked at her. He could begin to see her more. And they walked another day. He could see her more. The fifth night he could see her across the fire.

He said, "Tomorrow we shall be home." She looked at him. It was his joy to reach out. She was gone.

The shadow said, "Coyote, could you not wait one more night? Now she will never be with you."

"I will go back," said Coyote. "Now I know the way." The shadow was gone. The fire died down. Coyote slept.

Coyote started out, and soon he said, "Look what fine horses are running there." He held his hand up over his eyes.

Another day, he began to paw the air: "Let us bend down these branches and gather serviceberries for our meal." He chewed.

The fifth afternoon of his travel alone, he stood on the low hill where the dead had danced, where he had stood among them. He sat down to wait. The sun stood still, then it moved slowly, then it went down. Coyote tried to lift a flap of darkness away, to step forward. Then he waited again. Soon he would hear the dead sing. He would see their fires, he would walk from one to another. He would see the face of his wife.

He waited on the hill. It was dark. Nothing happened.

The students before me were very still. In my voice among them, Coyote was not a fool. The teacher looked at me hopefully. There was tremendous sorrow in the air. We did not know how to end the class.

I LEFT THE CAR at the rim of Joseph Canyon, and started down. A snow squall ended in sunlight, where elk bedded across a meadow ignoring me, and I followed their trails where my people had made none, down through pines that flavored the wind I sipped, rollicking through damp needle-duff with a swinging step all afternoon. Up on the rim, huge helicopters lifted whole trees from where the loggers had felled them— distant as dragonflies carrying twigs of grass. And I plunged down the slope.

The story is not what you do, but what fits. The story is not a sequence of actions, but a whole quilt unrolled in the storymaker's mind. My walk down Joseph Canyon was filled with sensation, with danger, meditation, discovery—pitch and smoke, rain down my back, a bed of rock at the top of Starvation Ridge. An owl called as I crossed the net of moonlight filtered through trees. By the charcoal of a fire, I found a book of camp songs the mice had chewed. I fed on nettle and fern root, and wood ticks fed on me. And I was lost three hours in the

snow, getting slowly chilled, afraid to sit down, tipsy with confusion, until I stepped abruptly out from the trees by the highway, and hitchhiked home.

NONE OF THAT was the story. No incident had enough of the
tight terror and swirl, the exhilaration of change. Pitch and
dragonfly, owl and moonlight, a cabin where no one lived for
years—those are fine in their way, but when I told the children
at Wallowa School, they all got righteously bored. I could tell
by how they got polite. They folded their hands. One glanced
at the clock. Another got interested in the boots I wore. So I
asked them to tell me about what it was like when they
were old. In the third grade, this is an easy task. They told me
without fear. One paper I carried away told this:

I WAS OLD

God woke up and he herd a Dinusor but
he was old and he sed to myself how
come he am in The old day how come
he don't no why and then I died and
he died for a little while and then he
came out of my graveyard and he
went back to sleep and he died
again and he woke up and Then
he was young and he Loved to dy
young and The End.

Vicki was the quiet one. She could be Coyote's wife. And, the
end. But there were seven minutes before the class was done. I
remembered one more little thing from Joseph Canyon—the
time I bent down to drink. It was the smallest moment, but
Vicki's story about being old made me know something, and I

started to tell it anyway. This time, the children forgot about me and listened to the story itself:

IT WAS A HOT DAY, and I was clear at the bottom of Joseph Canyon—hadn't taken enough water. But Joseph Creek, you know it's a big muddy torrent this time of year with a couple of cow pies floating by every so often. I wasn't going to take a drink of that.

Well, pretty soon I came to a little stream flowing in from the side—clear little stream about a foot wide—and I bent down to fill my hat. Water was real cool on my hands as I dipped the hat in, but as I stood up, a whole story went through my head. You know how fast a story can flash past your mind? It's a story my parents told me, sitting on the couch at home, when I was just a little guy:

Once upon a time there was a king, and this king liked to hunt, liked to take his hawk on his arm and ride out looking for game. He would send that hawk up to circle around until it saw a little rabbit, or maybe a quail, and then the hawk would swoop down and grab that little critter and bring it back.

Well, this one day it was pretty hot, and they weren't doing too well. Hadn't caught a thing. So they were riding home, with the hawk on the king's arm, and the king on the horse's back, just trotting along through the dust and hot wind. And this king gets real thirsty. Comes to a cliff where the water is dripping down, sends the hawk up to circle around while he holds his silver cup—kings always carry a silver cup, even to the hunt— holds his silver cup up to the water that drips and drips and drips. And just when he brings the cup that's full of this cool water up to his lips, the hawk swoops down and knocks it out of his hand and spills the water.

Hawks get kind of wild sometimes, and the king, being a king, isn't the kind of guy who just gets mad over any little thing, so he waves off the hawk, picks up the silver cup, and holds it up to the dripping water again. Well, the hawk circles above, the man holds his cup—even though his arm's about to fall off, he's so tired—and the water drips, and drips, and drips, and drips. And he sort of looks up at the hawk and tries to bring the cup up to his lips real fast—but the hawk is faster, swooping down and knocking the cup out of his hand again and spilling that water.

This time the king gets real mad, and he whips out his sword. Holds his cup up to the water again, and it drips, and drips—and this time when it's only half full he thinks he can fool that hawk, and he brings the cup up to his lips. But the hawk's too fast—swoops down, knocks the cup out of his hand, spills the water, and he swings his sword and kills that hawk with one blow.

By now this king is so thirsty, he can't wait to let that water drip again. So he drops his sword and his cup by the hawk, and he climbs up that cliff, and there at the top, sure enough, is a little pool where the water comes from. And just as he bends down to drink, his eyes see past the reflection of his face in the pool to where a snake lies dead in the water, sort of turned over on its side—a poison snake his hawk, circling above, had seen. The hawk had saved his life.

Then the story gets very sad. The king climbs down the cliff, takes up his hawk and folds its wings, wraps it in his crimson cape lined with gold, and rides home slow. . . .

But there I was with my hat in my hand just standing up to drink when that whole story goes through my head. And that story makes me hesitate just for a moment. I think about that story, and the water soaking out cool through my black felt hat and running down my elbows. And as I hesitate, the wind—which had been coming down the canyon behind me—shifts around to the side a little, and I smell this terrible smell. Just a little whiff, but awful. Just a little touch in my nose.

Instead of drinking, I dump the water out of my hat, shake it out, and walk up that little stream past a screen of pine saplings—and there, not thirty steps upstream, a dead elk lies across the water, hot and rotten, covered with flies. Been there for days. And now, when I look close at the water flowing in the little stream, I can see the rainbow sheen of some poison riding that water down toward where I dipped my hat.

And then I think to myself, if I had not remembered that story, I would have drunk the water, and never climbed out from Joseph Canyon.

The bell had rung. The buses had pulled up outside to take us home. "Remember your stories," I said. "They can save your life, a little at a time."

GRACE LIVES TOO FAR from town to worry when the snow falls deep. Can't drive? Stay home. But today the road is clear. As we step from the car, the colt hangs back, but her three Appaloosa mares crowd the barbwire fence stapled from tree to tree—aspen leaves just coming out. Bending to step between the second and third strands of wire, Grace says, "I guess a man goes over a barbwire fence, a child under, and a woman through. Glad you came out. Tea?" She gestures toward a mobile home hunched low into the ground, with a drift of gray leaves piled around the door.

Inside, bookshelves cover the walls.

"I've read them many times." Her hand sweeps the room. "The kind of snow we get is good for the mind." She turns around once and sits down. Her chair used to be red. Now it's covered with a faded quilt. "I'm kind of the unofficial historian of this place. I've got the books and got the time. People trust me with things, and I take care of them. Been to the museum? Sure you have! That's when I asked you to stop by. Have a seat!" We face each other across a formica table. Through the window, tiny aspen leaves flicker in sunlight.

"You said there is a tribe of people," I say, "living in Joseph Canyon."

"Oh yes, the hippies. Wanted to get away, I guess, and that's away! No one sees them, but everyone knows they're there. And you know, they found something. Got to digging around, disturbing one of the campsites, you know, and came up with a little stone carved to the shape of a bear. They kept it for a while, then got to feeling guilty I guess. Got to feeling bad about digging it up. So they took it back to where they'd found it. Tied a note to it. Left it there. My friend found that. He brought it to me.

"It was a bear carved out of basalt, a little one curled up asleep. It was a magic thing in your hand. You wanted to hold it forever. You wanted to hold it, and at the same time it didn't feel right to hold it. It belonged to the ground, to them, you know, to the people we drove away.

"I kept it for a while, then I sent it to the state museum, with a note asking them to give me some information on it and send it back. I thought they might have something similar, or some book that could tell me about it. But you know, they never sent it back. They never even wrote back. I got the idea they didn't trust me with it. We're just country people, you know. Left me bitter, I'm afraid. Left a bad taste in my mouth. I'd go bury it in the ground again, if I could."

The kettle boiled, and she got up to shut off the stove. Wind pushed wide the flimsy door, framed in aluminum, and sunlight burst across the rug covered with dog hair. Grace stood a moment with the kettle steaming in her hand.

"Things get lost, but then things get to be stories, I guess. And stories stick to people like cockleburs." She left the door open, held up a cup. "You take it black?"

DECEMBER MEDITATION
AT CAMP POLK
CEMETERY

YOU HAVE TO LISTEN real hard to hear anything at all: a little snow ticking down through juniper trees; the click of the chain around a family plot flexing in the cold. Wind. You hear it quite a while before it arrives. Then the eastern half of your face might just as well be stone.

Ten years ago I was here to do a formal study of the cemetery layout. As part of my folkloristic fieldwork, I made a systematic ramble of thirteen central Oregon cemeteries, stepping respectfully in the August dust of memorial plots at Grizzly, Antelope, Ashwood, Grandview, Madras, Hay Creek, Bakeoven, Warm Springs, Simnashio, Camp Polk, and three without names. I wanted to know how the adjacent communities of the living marked, laid out, and maintained these trim little cities of stone and sage. I wanted to know how many gravemarkers listed family relations, military ranks, professions, hobbies, wise proverbs, and the verses of grief or hope. I wanted to know how these stretches of sacred ground were isolated from the forest or cattle range surrounding them: wood fence, iron gate, barbed wire, poplar tree square. On the main street of how many towns would there be a sign for the "Cemetery: 2 miles"? How many plots would be local secrets tucked away up a side canyon?

I wanted to seek and listen, to map and ponder the visible artifacts of religious belief my people hold. I did all that. The study is in the archive. The memory works on me.

But now it's dusk at Camp Polk, and I'm visiting old friends. Here's Ray, by the champion juniper gnarl he loved to paint. His name in my mouth brings up a riff of banjo jangle I heard him play. There's a snow-swirl dancer over his place now.

I remember my discovery ten years ago, that graves everywhere planted heads to the west. This marks a Christian readiness to rise up facing Christ as He will bloom from the east on Judgment Day. And I remember how many of the thirteen cemeteries marked the end of a dead-end road: the Ashwood plot up a dirt track with no sign. The Grizzly cemetery at the ripe heart of a wheatfield with no road at all, forgotten like the town of Grizzly itself, which some prosperous corporation had bought. I drove around and around that field, knowing I was close, my map fluttering from my hand in the heat, until finally I squinted my eyes past the shimmering wheat and saw the cemetery fence out there roadless in the middle of the standing grain.

Somewhere near the cemetery here at Camp Polk, a hundred

odd years ago, the U.S. Army buried a cannon before fleeing from the Indians. Treasure hunters have sought it, as if it were a memory they owned by rights, as if that brass body might be raised up and carried away. You have to brave a series of "No Trespassing" signs to get to Camp Polk. Ten years ago there was a sign to invite visitors on toward the cemetery on its little hill beyond the most handsome of falling barns. This evening, there is no sign. You have to know.

Driving into Shaniko, on my cemetery route in 1975, I remember slowing the car to ask directions of an old-timer crumpled easily beside a shed, whittling steadily at a stub of wood. I didn't realize until too late the impertinence of my opening question: "Excuse me, sir, could you direct me to the cemetery?"

There was a tremendous pause, as he turned slowly up from his work to unroll a vacant smile. No answer was on the way. I thanked him, and drove on to the Eat Cafe. This time, I tried to be a bit more discreet, making my request in hushed tones to the waitress as she came rollicking across the room with half a dozen steaming plates along her arms.

"Excuse me, I'm trying to find the cemetery — for research."

She lurched expertly to a stop without jostling a plate, and shouted to the long table of white-haired ladies at the far end of the room, "Hey girls, we got a cemetery?" They vaguely shook their heads.

"Mister," she said, "we ain't got one. Try Antelope." I explained that I had already been there, and learned what I could.

"Well," she said, "then I don't think we can help you. We don't figure to do much dying in *this* town."

IF YOU LIE on your back to watch the snow come down, you will hear little rustlings in the grass, and you seem to see a long way up into the sky. You can try to be as still as everyone else, as hopeful and content.

I remember the gravestone at Agency Plains, the one with the sheriff's badge carved deep into the marble beside one name. Neighbors told me later he had never been Sheriff, but that was his life-long wish. Deputy, yes. Sheriff, never. Until then.

Religion in the desert has a lot to do with patience, and patience has a lot to do with silence. Beyond my feet where I lie at Camp Polk, there is a stone with an infant's oval ceramic photograph fixed to the pedestal. Someone sometime has used it for target practice, and the gray print of the bullet shies away low and to the left. There are so many children, and they are all so silent they are a chorus. The desert is big enough to hold that wind.

At Ashwood in that ten years back I heard a wind coming. All was still where I crouched, but I heard that wind. Hot. There was a permanence to every stone crumb and weed-stalk in the little enclosure of wire where I stood up. About a quarter mile away, a single tree was moving. The others were still. I folded my map and put it away. Then the little whirlwind moved down the hill into another tree and left the first tree alone. There was a weight to the afternoon. Then all the trees were still and the wind was a slender spiral of dust coming down toward me.

Even under the snow I can see the varieties of hope at Camp Polk: the ring of stone, the chain perimeter, the lichen-shredded picket fence, concrete moat, rusted cast-iron rail around a rich man's plot. In the sweep of open desert ground, the grave plot is a pouch, a box, a small fenced span of certainty. That's all. That's enough. It's nearly dark.

As I rise up, fervent and happy for every movement I make, snow shakes off my coat into my body's print on the ground. There is one thing still I must do. One of Camp Polk's oldest stones has fallen from its pedestal. Carved on the stone are the twin gates of heaven thrust wide. An orange swathe of lichen has covered the spirit's name. I can see only a submerged swirl of graceful lettering where the stonecutter engraved a name, a year, a lamb, and a verse.

I bend to lift the stone back into place, but it is frozen to the earth. I try to kick it loose, but my toes go numb. Then I see the initials. Chipped ruggedly at the base of the stone, never intended to be seen once it had been fit forever to the pedestal, are the stonecutter's secret letters "J.A.W.O.S." What for immortality? Public proclamations are prey to time. Only the secrets survive.

Was it at Grizzly? Was it at Hay Creek: the nameless stone sunk almost gone into the earth, with its moss-word "Mother"? Or was that Warm Springs, among the gifts of favorite things, the scattered trinkets love makes us give back to a place where we believe?

Good night, Ray. Bit windy, wouldn't you say? One thing about snow, though. It don't ever last.

A WALK
IN EARLY MAY

SOLITUDE is the scientific method of the human spirit. If you decide to fast, a full day and its night will be one arc of experience. If you decide not to take a map or to follow a trail, the path you make through broken country will be a chain of sensations. If you decide to take no warm covering for the night, you will change with the world, from warm and light, to cold.

South of Eureka lies a coastal country now dangerous with marijuana farmers and their guerrilla ways, with federal agents marauding in infrared helicopters and armored jeeps. But that was years away. I was there before, without a map, without food. I left the car and walked out onto the beach. The air was hot and still. The waves were an old rhythm beside me. I knelt over flat sand, where the tallest wave had sorted a ribbon of shell. Some four-footed creature had been along, leaving a trail that turned aside, as mine did, for every cluster of debris, every drift-bundle in the sand. One clear print told me it had been a coon, with two little ones. Inside the print, a gray scorpion the size of a ladybug was turning in a pirouette with its hands together. I was already hungry enough to understand that much.

In the midday shimmer, two women were talking in the waves. I turned: two seals, their eyes and whiskers level with the slick pelt of the water that rose and fell, rose and fell with a whisper. Not fear or purpose: a gentle curiosity came between us. An invitation to know. When they disappeared, kelp swirled from rocks that punctured the surface. I sat on the hot sand a long time. Then they came up, one little one bobbing behind them. This time they did not look at me. In seal, this was a compliment. The swell rose and they were gone again. Like the rocks, they had shown between waves; like the water, they had flowed away.

I walked south from the car, because it was easier to walk than decide. After a time, it was easier to stop. The inland dune glittered white above the tide-line. I held my hand above my eyes. It was a midden, a packed hill of rotted shell where the Indians had opened clams together. Generations of cockles to make one human life; generations of those lives to make a low hill waves had begun to carve. When I climbed it, deer in the meadow beyond bounded away into the blue-flowered scrub.

The hillside where the deer had fled was steep above the cove. The old ones had a narrow place to be happy together. Rocks clucked at the sliding water, the seals spoke now and then. There was a great distance in a small space. Before my face where I lay down, wind made the tiny seeds of the grass sway where they were tethered.

I walked south in the trance of heat, at the rim of hunger. Walking was what the wind did, the sun. It had nothing to do with destination. Not a plan, but a way of being. Where I stopped, the seals were clustered offshore, bobbing in the water between two arms of rock. I was a stranger. They were older with the place. I lay down on the sand, my arms tight to my sides, my feet together. Became a shape for water. They murmured and came closer. They climbed onto the rocks. The curiosity came between us. All about me on the sand were the curved prints of their bodies where the tide had beached them high, where they had slept a while, then elbowed down to the water. Now they said one syllable with all its inflections—*oh, oh, oh, oh*—from deep in the body. The seals go down into another world, then come back to tell that.

Behind the beach was another midden, the white strata of shell deep in the bank waves had opened, had spilled. The bright slope I climbed was littered with whole, old abalone shell, each moon-shape just shy of full, with a curved line of bubbles spiraling out from where it began. Clamshell crumbled like ash under my feet, and the white bone too long to not be whale-rib flaked away when I bent to touch it.

My hand closed over a hammerstone: a cylindrical shape with a rim at the top for my first finger to curve under. The striking face at the bottom was worn down by shell of clam and shattered acorn. It was heavy, hot like the sand it came from, just the blunt, thick shape of a man. It was a tool of abundance even as it opened a hull or shell. The works of food and pleasure had a single way in this stone; each motion with it was a blessing.

Somewhere up the hill, in a private midden of their own, the bones of the maker lay. I climbed the white slope, my shoes filling with sand. Above, on the uneroded midden roof, a fawn lay still, bunched on its side as if running, the small black hooves joined to the leg-bones in a white articulation repeated in the multiple curve of rib, the compact flex of spine, in the skull turned back over the shoulder, the small jaw open. It moved yet it did not. It slept, more than slept. Coyote would have scattered the bones. It must have been vulture or crow pared away all color from it, all flesh.

Where I knelt in the grass to know this, at the tip of a grass stem, the flat, round body of the tick reached yearning toward me. I held my finger out. She clung to the grass with two feet, the other six flailing the air. I was the prey, she the predator courting me, embrace aching in her arms. In the old tale it was Coyote who heard the tick call, "Darling, darling, will you marry me?" And then the tick climbed onto his back and they walked away. Soon, the tick was the greater of the two. Soon, Coyote clung to a twig and called to travelers, "Darling, darling, will you marry me?" Things are powerful in proportion to their smallness. This one came blindly onto my finger, not now in haste, having found the broad landscape of desire, to begin the deep kiss that fulfills her life. There is one feast; all are invited. The clam, the fawn, the crow. The tick, the shaper of the stone.

But the two of us would be hungry for a time. With a buttercup leaf I brushed her gently to the ground, still thin, still stirring her eight short filaments for knowing. She found the base of a tall stem and began to climb. The sun was hot on my shoulders. I felt the cramp in my knees and stood.

To the north, my car was a grain of light. The sun had gone into mist over the long waves, a haze that rose up in plumes of gray. I sat a while by a drift log above the water. Far up past the beach, over the ridgetop a hawk was hovering low. Maybe, if I climbed there and lay in the grass, the hawk would come back along the spine of meadow, unsuspecting, and be close above my face, its wings open just over my mouth. I had learned to stand up slowly now.

The slope was steep, perhaps dangerous to one in a hurry. There was no path at first, and I climbed with the speed of the blind. My feet had to know first, and balance was more than direction. Where the slope quickened, I hunched aside into a small cave. On the ceiling, swallows had made their nests of mud like beaded bags against damp rock. They were absent this season, and the nest-shapes were crooked throats. A bit of swallow down flickered at the mud rim of one. There was a line across the cave mouth: water's blue horizon.

The open slope narrowed to a slot between spicy bushes of a small blue flower, then to a thistle-arroyo, then to poison oak in a broad band, the blond flowers clustered on it sweet, its green leaves bright with oil. Where deer had shouldered through that thicket, I turned aside, went down on all fours under a wind-flattened fir, into the aisle of its shade so dark nothing grew. One tree was braided to the next, the lowest limbs shade-killed and rotten, dropping from my lightest touch as I crawled the dark tunnel upward. In this thicket of limbs, to be straight, to aspire, was death by wind. Side-limbs fattened into trunks, until the trees joined by the rub and link of long limbs, their pitch-wounds sealed in the cambium weld.

Smaller than aphids, red bugs dusted my hand. A centipede, stone-gray, flowed over a crumpled limb, the lashes of its feet automatic as water. I crouched to watch its grace in the impossible maze of duff. It was the muse of travel, the patron saint of complexity. Past this solitude, beyond the dark interlaced limbs in silhouette, a meadow hummed with sunlight. Flattened on belly and knee, I flowed out from under the last limbs sweeping into the grass and rose up, vacant in the heat.

Steeper, but impossibly open and easy, the slope of grass and fern led me higher, as I switched back and forth along the quilted trails of the deer to stretch my muscles on either side. Wind hit the slope full force, gleaning away every loose crumb of soil or rock. Rain, frost-clench, seismic nudge made me a participant in scree. I balanced on a pebble, a tuft.

At the blunt brow of the ridge, I crept low to the peak; the wind was behind me, but my scent would be baffled by the updraft, and there could be deer or coyote dozing on the far falling slope. As I peered over, a stiff wind snatched back my breath. Beyond, through the tears buffeted from my eyes, was green, all green, a variety of shape and tone to hills and cleft ravines dividing them.

I rolled back into calmer air, spread my cramped legs and arms. Would the hawk swing down now? I sprawled on my back in the deep grass and slept.

I WAS A SHAPE stunned by sunlight, inert, compact, my motive exhaled and done. The sun spun through my head and chest; my four limbs lay flung out in limp vines, a dumb warmth in each leafy palm; my eyes were blank slots of sunlight. The sky hung above in a red dome. One shadow, another, crossed the dome in a flicker of blue. When I cracked open my eyelids, the air above me was thick with vultures wheeling close from the pivot of myself. I did not want to frighten them.

Be still. Know this as they do: first the eyes—by them confirm possession—then the softer flesh about the mouth, and then the rest with time as rot makes easy. I was afraid only of myself for thinking this—that I might scare them off by moving too soon, too soon to fully live out in mind the necessary accomplishment of my bones, as the fawn had lived it out, the abalone pried from certainty, the hand that made the round stone and left it.

But then of itself, my left hand twitched, and the broad forms of the vultures—nine, I counted now—rose from me, still silent as wind, and drifted off when my eyes came wide. Their calm was mine; we were patient with each other. Our etiquette was to have no fear. I was now awake.

I HAD NEVER SEEN the world. I was alive. Down the eastern slope, air was cooler, and light in a slant made every leaf testify, every stick and pebble stand bright as witness to itself. Where poison oak seemed to close my way, there was a ravine beckoning to the side. I sat on the shoulder of it, tried to know its poise. From the redwood to the bay tree, a bluebird made of song and flight one motion. There was a water-sound. The honey-colored ant explored my sleeve, slowing to a crawl at my wrist-fur. Inland, the great blue hills, the sky, loomed in a single color beyond the slot of the canyon where the ground dropped away. Tumbling from my finger, the ant set off through the grass with something white between its jaws. Something of me.

On the east slope I was now in shadow, and as I drifted across a steep meadow I saw the doe, curled asleep, twenty yards below me. I was blessed to see this. I had seen the bones of the fawn lie still. I had slept. I watched over the doe. After a time, she lifted her head slowly to watch the open country below, her wide ears spread away from where I crouched in fern. The wind was toward me, and only a sound or flicker of movement could startle her. A jay cried; the ears swiveled like broad leaves. A small bird sang long and easy; the doe's ears folded back behind her slender head.

She rose up, watched a moment for any response to her rising, then stretched and stepped out onto the open slope. Beside her, another doe rose up from the shade. The two stood, slightly oblique to one another, divided as the one's ears had been, to listen. They did not look my way, only below into the brushy ravines between shoulders of clear ground.

As they began to feed, their lips had the touch of small hands reaching into bunched leaves at the ground. The head of the first swung up toward me, as the other browsed. There was a design for knowing: the round eyes sprang open to each side, the nostrils flared forward, while the ears, veined and gray, spread like moth wings for flight. Her tail flashed white, then again, pleading with a predator to lunge in warning. I let my gaze drift slowly from that signal to a distant leaf: be native to this place, be harmless—a stump hunched gray, solid in the fern, with a wisp of lichen at the top. I had been a tree here a century alive and twenty winters after stripped by fire, wind-shattered, whitened in the sun. Fern spore had fallen into the rotted hollow of my throat, and moss held to the cool north side of my face, always damp, shaggy with dew. An ant crept across my rooted hand.

When my eyes, released from their trance, drifted into focus on the deer, they both were feeding. Soon, they had worked their way around the hill and were out of sight. Wind skittered through the ferns.

The bedded circles of the deer in shade were no longer warm to my hand, but the grass lay flat. Here, the morning sun would strike, the afternoon be cool; rising air all day would bring living scents from below, and uphill was nothing but open ground. This place was safe, for no one of this country crossed open ground in full sunlight. I sat a while myself there, looking over the world; the sun was low, and this slope was all bright shade. Bay trees in the ravine passed the wind one to another. The moon, in half, hung straight above. With the deer, it was time for me to move away into the evening. As I walked I began to break off the unraveled brush of the fern. I would need a bed somewhere. The deer were gone; I would not disturb them with my noise.

At the peak of the ridge again, under a fir I spread my arm-load of fern, then leaned branches from a windfall against each other to make a roof. Crooked sticks were best for this. They were strong two ways at once.

In the thin grass at the hilltop was a bronze survey-marker, a ring of numbers and words too dark to read. Four fallen fenceposts and a tangled strand of wire. I sat down. The sun had gone but the sky was bright. I would be warm for a time; a mosquito came singing.

With the first stars came the light-points of eight fishing boats far below on the flat Pacific. Some were anchored still; others wandered across the darkness. There in the sky above rambled the round constellation of the tick, its eight arms glimmering; there the starlight cluster of the fawn's bones. There among stars the vacant sack of the swallow's nest. There the alert triangle of the deer's head, listening. Slowly, the deer's face slid to the horizon; it became a curve, a seal diving without a word. A star fell burning across the west. The wind began to touch me with cold.

I turned toward my shelter of branches. Far to the east, too far for sound, above the distant light of a farm a human flare burned sudden in the sky, scattering out in fragments as it flashed and went dark. In both worlds, a disintegration by fire. Because I was awake with hunger and vulnerable with cold, I was afraid.

MY BODY had four sides. The side toward earth was warm. I lay on my back this time in the seventh turning. The crushed fern was soft, the wind cold. Moon was moving west, toward water, where it would make a path. Later, maybe, there would be an owl calling.

If I had rounded a stone with my hands, I would hold it now. The stone would not be mine, but its shape would belong in my hands. The stone would be cold as I was—not quite cold enough to shake. I was still; it was the tree that moved. An owl did call. I was not shaking yet. I had four sides, and one was warm. If I began to shake, I would turn partway. The seasons pass to keep the Earth alive. The owl was calling for this. I was cold now. Even the tree was still.

Something touched the earth—I felt it. Down the slope two deer were feeding; the darker clusters of their bodies moved against moonlit grass. I lay back. The sky. The tree. The owl calling. Something comes to one alone, not a song like honey is sweet. A song like water. I was cold and had not eaten; this was a part of it. How does the tree stand, even after it has died? We both lived. The moon was there; a moth flew toward it. The owl made a sound. A song is given in the place one lives. Even the tick, wordless with desire, knew this. The tree has a way, a secret way. Sometimes another may hear it. The seal dives to find out. I was cold; I was spared the fullness of it, knowing then my own. Something came to me shapeless. Then it had a shape and I belonged.

WHEN I HAD TURNED twenty-eight times, the fern grew thin and the darkness softened. These ways are nocturnal: the full blossoming of stars; a pilgrim's true solitude. As light came on, a clarity retreated from the world. A small bird was telling what it knew.

By the time I had picked my way downslope for an hour, the sun came to me and I was warm again, so filled with waking I felt no hunger. When I would eat, sometime soon, the precision to my witness of the earth would dwindle, as the tones of darkness dwindle at first light and are hard to remember. I lived on hunger for the time, and all forms lived with me—dew on the bay leaf swiveling from its twig, the vines of poison oak braided by light on a trunk of fir.

I came to a stream, then to the road. I saw the car at a great distance, a white glint of modern time. Beyond it, the waves came silently. I perched on a boulder broken from the road-cut. Soon I would balance on one foot beside the car and shed my clothes—the ones with poison oak brushed into them—and stand naked a moment. I would be cold. Then I would dress and it would go away.

Rain was driving in toward land, but where I stood was still. If this were a story, no rainbow could hang clean and various over the road; but this was my life, and the arc of the storm was there.

THE
SEPARATE
HEARTH

AFTER SCHOOL I stopped at home to change my outfit—
shucking my slacks for jeans, tossing aside my polite cotton shirt
for the buckskin one my grandmother had sewn, pulling on my
boots—and lit out for The Woods on the run. We called it *The
Woods*, just as we called a nearby slope *The Big Hill;* the lim-
ited territory of childhood is exact, and therefore mythic. Two
blocks from home the human world dwindled to a path threading through nettle and alder. A spider web across the path
meant no one was there before me. I crawled under its fragile
gate to solitude and was gone.

This was my routine from third grade to high school—to
straggle home after dark and stand in the cold garage, shivering

and balancing on one foot to shed my muddy clothes. It was a certain evening in my junior year that I realized with a shock I could walk directly into the kitchen; I had somehow not fallen—or leapt—into the creek, had not slithered up a mossy tree, hugging the trunk with my thighs and arms, or spilled down a bank of mud. I had politely walked in the woods and returned. I mistrusted my sincerity. Something had changed. Something had gone wrong.

"What did you find today?" my grandmother (we called her Boppums) would ask, as she sat picking at a crust of cockleburs in one of my socks. I would run to my mud-stiffened pants to dig through the pockets for a rock an Indian might have used, or a leaf I liked, crumpled and fragrant, or a waterlogged stick turning into a fossil, a furry length of twine I had braided from cedar bark.

"I could use this to snare a rabbit, if I had to."

The Woods was a wild tract developers had somehow missed in their swathe through old Oregon. It probably stretched about three miles long by two miles wide, and was surrounded by the city of Portland and its suburbs. Raccoon, beaver, salmon, deer, awesome pileated woodpeckers, and exotic newts were among the secret lives of the place. Once, in the fifth grade, four of us decided to head north through unexplored territory toward the edge of the world. Lewis and Clark had nothing on us, on our glorious bewilderment when we emerged, near dark of a long Saturday, to find a broad, dangerous road, a tall house covered with ivy, and a giant in blue coveralls mowing his lawn.

"Where are we?" Bobby Elliott shouted over the roar of the motor.

The man looked down at a row of muddy, scratched little savages. "Terwilliger Extension," he shouted. We were stunned to silence by this bizarre name for most of the long detour home, past the ice-cream store.

WHAT *DID* WE DO down there all those hours multiplied by weeks and years? When we went together, we often hatched a project—more like Robinson Crusoe than John Muir in our use of the wilderness:

"Let's find the charcoal-wagon boy's old road!"

"Let's find Indian relics!"

"Let's *make* Indian relics!"

"Let's go to the Old Mill and make a fort!"

"Let's wade as far as we can without stepping out of the creek—so no one can track us!"

"Let's roast a skunk cabbage root and try to eat it!"

"Let's make a path with steps in the hill and signs so an eighty-year-old woman could follow it!"

"Let's make elderberry pipes and smoke leaves!"

"Let's steal those real estate signs and hide them!"

Although our research into history, botany, anthropology, and geography almost got us poisoned or arrested on several occasions, we lived by joy. Once we ate a kind of wild carrot, then came home to look it up in Pat O'Shea's father's medical text. The only plant we could find of similar description was called *hemlock:* "A piece of the root the size of a walnut can kill a cow." I never read a sentence in school that had such impact. The dizzying image of a stricken cow lurching heavily to its knees will inhabit my brain whenever I am about to taste a new food. That time, we were spared.

When I went to The Woods alone, my experience was shaped by a book Boppums had given me, Theodora Kroeber's *Ishi in Two Worlds*. It told the story of "The Concealment," a last cluster of five Yahi Indians in northern California living in the mountains at a place they called *wowunopo*, "the grizzly bear's hiding place," and finally of Ishi himself, alone in an empty world. Like Ishi, I was the last man, the only man of a lost tribe. I too had a small, sacred geography hidden even from my friends. If America ended, I would be there in my shelter of boughs. A huge tree had fallen, and where the root-mass tore out from the earth a hollow was left that no one could see, roofed over with the arched limbs of fir, woven by my hands with sword fern and moss, with leaf litter, until the roof became a knob of the earth itself. Like Ishi, I approached by a different way each time, so as not to wear a path others might see, and I covered the entrance to my den with boughs broken, not cut in a human way.

Inside, I would kindle a fire—only along toward dark so the smoke could not be seen—and be utterly alone with it, staring into the flame, nudging twigs together as they crumbled into ash, then letting it die and stumbling home along the ways I had memorized, to shed my clothes in the garage, to find my dinner in the oven and the family dispersed for the evening around the house.

My apocalyptic fantasy was nourished by the Cold War that filled the time—the air-raid drills in grade school, the evasive answers by adults, their troubled looks and few words about the greatest terrors of our world. In seventh grade we cornered our history teacher in the hall and demanded, "Will the bomb fall?"

"No."

"How do you know?"

"If I thought it would, I couldn't live my life."

WHY DID BOPPUMS encourage my life in the woods that harvested so many cockleburs? She was a small, genteel woman, a minister's widow who stood humming at the ironing board while she watched a black and white *Edge of Night* on our tiny television. As a young bride, she had spent a desperate season trying to homestead in Wyoming, and she had few illusions about the glories of primitive life. Yet she had sewn this elaborately fringed buckskin shirt for me, and had given me my own bible of the primitive, *Ishi*, which taught me to be separate among my countrymen and distinct from my kindest friends, about wilderness skills and beliefs, about a kind of existential fortitude that could keep one alive when the universe is wrenched awry and all people die. What was her lesson for me?

I learned a lot in the kitchen, working with my mother and with Boppums around the stove. I called myself my mother's company-boy, the one who would be there to stir, or crack an egg, or knead, grease the pan, lick the beater, help wash up. I loved to pour the oil into the batter; then I could see down into the secret center through the amber window it made. And I loved to open the oven to slide a toothpick into brown bread, my face hot, lungs filled with a nourishing fragrance of steam. This was the hearth where the family would gather when the bread was done to cut the first crust away, butter it, divide it. There were many lessons beyond the recipe.

Once when I came home from The Woods my mother

stared hard at my face. "What happened to you? You look different! Your eyelashes are gone!"

I had to admit they were. I explained that I had begun to build my fire, but it wouldn't catch. As I knelt over the tinder to blow, it suddenly flared about my face. My hair crackled in an acrid smoke, and my face felt like the sun, but I fell back unhurt.

My parents discussed the use of matches—both at this point, and later, when Van Dusenbery and I tied my sister to the tetherball pole and *pretended* to burn her at the stake. My parents decided I could continue to carry matches, if I would promise to be careful. I promised, both times.

But why were the matches, kept dry in a slim match-safe with a screw-cap in my pocket, such an essential part of my get-up that I dared not venture forth without them? Of course, there was my motto as a Boy Scout: Be Prepared. "For what?" one might ask. But that's not how the saying goes—just Be Prepared. Carrying matches, and a knife, and some string, and a book in case I got bored, and a dime, and a magnifying glass, a stub of hacksaw, a little measuring tape that rolled into itself, and other tools that made my pockets bulge was the way I lived. I sauntered so equipped to school, to The Woods, and even to the city where I went for my clarinet lesson. I really needed a purse for it all, and I envied girls the amount of private stuff they could carry in the big handbags of the time. I finally made myself a bag from the waxy canvas covering of a war-surplus life preserver and trudged to school with it slung over my shoulder. Not fire, not a carving, but the ability to make fire, to cut, to tie things into a bundle—these were what Boppums and Ishi, and my parents, and my own sense of fear and mission in the world had taught me.

"If you are lost and have a knife," my father said, "you can make anything you need. First whittle a figure-four to catch a rabbit; then from rabbit sinew, braid a bowstring, and carve your bow from a yew limb. Then with the bow catch a deer, and make a coat from the skin. *Then* you'll be snug."

What a strange message to give a child. Now I remember that my father himself was alone like that during World War II—a conscientious objector isolated in a camp in northern California with other dissidents, fighting fires and planting trees in the very mountains Ishi roamed. My father felt the dangers, and the exhilaration of such isolation, and its required self-reliance. One time he was nearly hung by a mob made bold by wartime frenzy. And when the bomb fell, and the rest of America shouted and rang bells, he looked at his friends in confusion. And my mother, with her beautiful smile and her one good hand—did she feel alone in the world, for all her grace and articulate success? And Boppums, her mother, who gave me the book that somehow told our story? Did they, together, silently, teach me to be Ishi, to be a pacifist Hansel with no crumbs, to be a monkish "soldier of the cross," to be a bear boy gone far from others to live alone and discover from scratch what being a true spirit in a wild place might mean?

In the woods by myself, fire was the heart of it all. In my secret den, or in some refuge off the trail—in The Moss Forest, on The Island, beside The Stockade, on the sand beside The Second Creek, or near The Spring—I would seek out the low, shade-killed twigs of a hemlock tree, and the ritual of isolation and sufficiency would begin. I would hold a broken branch to my lips to see how dry it was. The lips, not the fingers, could tell. I would lay a ring of stones dug into mineral soil and arrange perfect sticks one over the other. I would slip out one match from the gleaming steel safe in my pocket, peel off the paraffin cap from its head with my thumbnail, and shield the hearth with my body from the wind—this the repeated prelude to my identity. When the match burst open in my cupped hands, and the flame climbed obediently through the precise architecture of my kindling, I had made, again, my own portable world in the world. The small fire talked, it warmed, it required care and responded well, it made me smell smoky and wild, and as evening darkened around us its coals were the small landscape of my thought.

Here was my private version of civilization, my separate hearth. Back home, there were other versions of this. I would take any refuge from the thoroughfare of plain living—the doll-house, the treehouse, the hidden room under the stairs, the closet, tunnels through furniture, the tablecloth tent, the attic, the bower in the cedar tree. I would take any platform or den that got me above, under, or around the corner from the every-day. There I pledged allegiance to what I knew, as opposed to what was common. My parents' house itself was a privacy from the street, from the nation, from the rain. But I did not make that house, or find it, or earn it with my own money. It was given to me. My separate hearth had to be invented by me, kindled, sustained, and held secret by my own soul as a rehearsal for departure.

Is this a necessity for education—that each child must have

some kind of separate hearth, some separate fire to kindle in secret? My friends had their own small worlds I knew a little about. They would spend their private hours under the hood of a car, or between earphones of the Grateful Dead. To make a dead car speak is akin to the miracles we are asked to perform in adult life. To kindle pleasure in a lover's body, to kindle a vision in the mind through drugs—these were the forbidden ways some chose. For each of my friends, the separate hearth might be alcohol, religion, TV, crime. Theft and vandalism were ways of knowing and proving. Most went out on some kind of vision-quest in those days. Some didn't come back clear. But some never went at all, and these were the ones who obeyed only voices from outside themselves.

The world did end. My friends died, or changed, sold out, moved away. They became their parents or hurt their parents. Today my own clothes are clean. I walk in through the front door and leave no tracks. My pockets are flat. I carry money and a comb. I carry a driver's license with my picture on it. I don't carry matches to my clarinet lesson. I don't even play the clarinet. So what did Boppums teach? What did the fire teach? What is Ishi to me now, and how am I made ready by my years at the hearth hidden in the dark woods?

My first answer came when I heard Boppums falter, heard her suffocation-cough, alone with the doctor where she had collapsed in my sister's room. I heard my mother cry somewhere far off in the house. My father was trying to comfort her. And I held my little sister, telling her the lies of my wish.

"She will be all right. Isn't the doctor there? Don't let her hear you cry!" But Boppums was hearing nothing then.

That time, we were the ones to stay behind, while she went on alone.

TWENTY YEARS passed before my turn came, and a kind of light filled my body, though I lay in our dark tent at six thousand feet, my eyes closed, my brother beside me and the last flash of lightning sizzling away to thunder. I knew. I knew I was about to die. The next bolt would run down the tree above us and blast through our bodies into the ground. The light began in my head, then flowed out along the ravines and caves of my chest, arms, legs. The glow within me meant I was chosen, perhaps my brother, too. There was no need to wake him. It would be too soon.

As I remember that moment now, I wonder why it didn't happen, why the glow within me faded to darkness and the storm passed without staking me to the earth with flame. Gripped by expectation of death—it was a fact, not a possibility—I had felt utterly easy. I had felt a joy beyond success. I had seen that moment as a gift to me, had known with brilliant clarity my brother beside me, my sister's husband in the next tent, the tree dead but standing above us, my wife and child distant and spared. I had visited—no, I had become the separate hearth. I had suddenly fit into history and been content.

As the storm passed, I needed to know what the fact of my death could mean for my life. How should I talk now, matured by this fact? How should I drive, or cook, or pay taxes? Was I still an American, a member of the twentieth century? I had to reach back somewhere and answer.

After Boppums died, after my mother reported from the

funeral, one of my needs was to step outside after dark. The street light would be there, courted by moths; the moon would be above me, or a tree or ragged cloud. One of my needs then was to look back at the pod of the house from a distance—say, from across the school ground, or from the top of the water tower I had climbed. That house down there was the compartment of human life, was the world Boppums made so calm, but she was gone and I was gone. I had been borne outward.

NOW THE MATCH-SAFE I carry must be something about memory. With memory, with words I whittle and bind, hide, magnify, kindle—kindle the path beyond the spider web. Kindle the stump-cave with its roof of fern. Kindle the log high up over the creek, the ribbon of certainty my feet knew by dark. I kindle Boppums who died. I cup my hands around the soft light of her face. At the sink, I wash my daughter's face. "What did you find today?"

Boppums made me a leather shirt, then sent me somewhere she could never see. Grandmother, mother, daughter—I learn so slow: part of our love must be to teach each other how to live alone.

PINE,
FIR,
CEDAR,
YEW

MY WORKBENCH is a writhing bundle of stories. It sports salty driftwood that crossed the pond, and salvage boards from the day they leveled my sister's house. By a trestle up the Gorge, I plucked for a shelf a clear fir stair-tread that flipped off a train. Another shelf is the sweet pine plank pulled clean from the Camp Sherman dump, and my hand slaps the stub-beam worktop one penitent carpenter dropped off before dawn. He owed us money, but paid us in boards. By wood's magic, that bench fits. On it, I saw pine, plane fir, chisel cedar, split yew. Shavings curl fragrant from the plane iron, as I delve into wooden years. This is like joining words: the material has centuries on the carpenter. Best be humble. Working so, I will learn history as a tree knows it. When the tree is my teacher, I will set the tool aside for a time to simply make hymns of stories. I will make of concentric memory a stem of praise. I will be the traveler who stays, patriot to this ground. Now choose the tree of life, said my dream. Choose the living Maypole woven of green and sunlight, rooted to earth.

Heartwood burns for stories. A pioneer left his rifle in the crotch of a willow sapling; after fifty years, only the tip of the barrel and the butt of the stock were visible. Horseshoes, nailed up for luck, were lost by the score to the hearts of trees, and later played hell with sawmill saws. While we lived in the house that later burned, my father kept a list of the woods that fed our stove—mostly driftwood from the Tualatin River. When I was three, their names grew dense in my heart like a habit of virtue. They were a pantheon of pious and thorny relatives rattling in the woodbox, speaking from the stove. That list was simply the best literature of the alphabet:

ash	black walnut	cedar	apple
oak	hawthorn	poplar	maple
willow	locust	holly	pine
cottonwood	hazel	fir	yew

Wood has a way of harvesting centuries into itself, and holding the years compact. The girth of a tree is visible time. When my father sawed through the crotch of a locust log, I touched the double wedding ring that can't be split. It was gold, but fragrant. In our yard I watched time and light spin trees. Every gnarl or burl or branch grew right. This was architecture.

Only my sturdy grandmother was a ruin graceful as a tree. She withered like wood, and she grew smaller, we thought—closer to the right size.

In a tale from the Brothers Grimm, the mother condemned the old man, her father, to eat from a wooden bowl. He would drop no more china with his palsied hands, she said. He ate alone from his trencher then, sitting apart on his wood stool on the wood floor in the wood house in the dark forest of the old. One day the little grandson began to whittle by the hearth.

"What do you make, my dear young son?"

"Mother, I make a wooden bowl for you. When I am big, you will be too old to eat from china."

And the mother said, "Oh my son, oh my father."

Trees shall heal us; wood shall soften our ways. In one parable, not in the Bible, Jesus says, "Turn over the stone, and you will find me; cleave wood and I am there." What holds the Holy of Holies, what did Brahma become? Wood. Why will aspen always tremble? For the nails driven into the cross. What makes the color of wood? The soil it tastes. In Mexico, the tree called primavera is cut in the dark of the moon, when the sap is down. Cradle, fiddle, coffin, bed: wood is a column of earth made ambitious by light, and made of beauty by the rain. "Praise simply the tree that lives," an old man said; "do not think so fast what else to make of it."

The old builders hewing cedars of Lebanon, the carvers of applewood, the toilers who rive pine into clapboards, and roughened hands polishing a spruce pole with sand—all have a beautiful knowledge. The ways of teaching trees to be boards are older than steel. Before steel, the Kwakiutl adz of jade. But even with sharp steel, the question remains: who is the real teacher, tool or wood? The yew has a right, the pine has a healing wish. There still stands one deep grove: four hundred cedars of Lebanon. I would be apprentice now to the wood, not to the tool. I would ask, what can a pine tree teach me? What will fir remember? What lore fills the scent of cedar, the twang of yew spoken by the living branch?

WHEN I WALKED into the woodyard with Ward, he knew at a glance which boards had grown in the West. His finger went out: "That's western black walnut—nice brown play. That's eastern: closer grain, and no figure to speak of. Lot simpler to work the eastern: find the downhill run for your plane, and you get a long curl. Your western—now quarter, rift, or flat-sawn board—you'll fight chips all day, but what a face!"

The upshot is this, as Ward told me: west coast trees grow faster. The season for growth stretches out, and spring's earlywood ring runs wide, followed each year by an ample band of the denser latewood of summer. Long, hungry growth makes a rich ripple pattern for western boards. The grain in a flat-sawn plank tends to run wild, to show the moiré of abundant light. And in the Northwest, the wood-grain figure plays marionette to mild rain threaded down from Oregon clouds early as March, when leaves first explode, and deep into October. In the East, balance prevails. The tight, dark wait of a longer winter corsets the heartwood, slows growth to a crawl, and yields a grain that tends to play out even, classical.

I've met workers since who scoff at this guessing. They say it's bluff to claim Ward's regional code for a board. Soil, exposure, crowding, and the sheer genetic pluck of certain trees make the figure in a board, not geography. I'm gullible. I will believe them about wood. Perhaps origin east or west is a minor fact for a board. But I will graft Ward's belief to people. Don't Westerners grow fast and show the wild figure of abundant light?

Believers, Ward and I leafed through planks as if we were loose in the library stacks, reading the lives of trees: bole, knot, heart, pith, checked crotch, cup and wind, figured grain and spalted punk. Here were boards ripped out kerf on kerf by the gang saw, then bundled back into whole logs book-matched for symmetry. I learned the plain complexion of a board has many names. A freshly opened log can thrill with dimple, mottle, bee-wing figure, blue stain, burl. Trouble for a tree often makes the most compelling figure in a board. Spiral grain from windstress gives a rare ribbon figure highly prized in certain woods. But some injuries leave the board flawed: brash failure, heart shake, wane. I touched a ten-foot flitch of pearwood, edges feathered out in bark. Wood starts warm against the hand. It has fed on sugar all its life.

In a corner of the yard, I had my moment with the flitch of pear. Wood gives back to the knowing hand a musical note. Be intimate. Every plank has a resinous presence, a life splayed visible. Savor the figure by eye, the ripple of its restless growth by hand. Heft it like a dancing partner. Spin it on end to sight its length for twist. If it's thin enough to give, flex it for spring. Lay fingers to its face then, and stroke for grain: does it splinter raw, fuzz out, soften? Rap with your knuckles to sound its timbre. Is it self-possessed? Lean close, chin to grain: inhale. Is life there still, blond pear, the odor of cedar, walnut's bite, applewood sweet as bread, rank pine? Touch lip to the wood. Is it damp? Will it season well, or was it cut too thin too soon? Will it check or wind, cup or bow?

Ward pulled hardwoods. He does law firms and opulent waiting rooms. He sculpts mahogany banisters to lead the supplicant up corporate stairways. He carves chairs and credenzas, sunburst conference tables that stun in walnut and oak with a purfle of brass. He works in rosewood buffed to a shine, in ebony from India. He joins furniture tough enough to forget the punishment of use, and sometimes too graceful to be used at all. These pieces have returned to the state of sacred trees.

Behind his swathe, I touched and savored the thrifty Oregon woods that grow fast and remember everything—the light sanded pine I could score with a thumbnail, rusty heartwood fir rippled with planer marks, fragrant cedar dressed by the spinning turmoil of the saw, and a heavy yew bolt for bows. Ward's boards filled a cart. I was not in the mood to acquire, but to remember. My hands came out of the woodyard empty, but my head filled with the pantheon of pine, fir, cedar, yew.

PINE, whitebark pine is a soft, light wood designed to hold up trees. Once, on Strawberry Mountain, when I was honed by hunger and alone, I sat by one isolated tree to learn what I could. A tree like that is kin to me, is intimate without the keen distraction of a face. It stood, or rather hunched, more like lightning's path than a stem. In silhouette against stone, it twitched for occasional wind. Something graceful in this wood soul beckoned me to remain, to settle on a flat stone and confer in the dialect of tree. I asked my brothers to go on down to Hidden Lake. I would follow, after a time. In an afternoon, that stunted, five-needle whitebark pine had twenty-seven lessons for me:

Pine stands limber in its bones. Every fiber holds, and gives.

There is a way to heal yourself alone. Pine's life is a constant healing urge.

Pine stands older, but shorter. This is my first lesson about humility, about the smaller ambition of pure life.

Pine has not a mind for prophecy, but a concentric memory, its earliest youth clenched at the heart.

Pine's blood is fragrant. My hands stick together like prayer: bitter sugar of its life.

Visible pine is rooted to an equivalent unseen self. While the limbs seek light, the roots seek water—never so much as a chickadee's sip, but simple wet. That unseen self is no ghost; that dreaming mind is gritty, actual, anchor.

Pine is not powered by a busy heart, but by the seasonal pump of earth, by the long need and suck of transpiration, the tidal year-throb of change.

Pine is born to a cleft in stone, and makes the most of it. Whitebark is most primitive: the cones must rot before the seeds can split and live. As in the parable, one fell here on stony ground. Unlike the parable, this tough seed lived anyway.

When wind blows, travel in place. Trade the gypsy-foot for residence. This means the impossible acrobatic persistence of a limb toward light.

Pine nourishes the clump of sweet duff that nourishes it. Above eight thousand feet, there is an abundance of time, but not of soil. After half a dozen winters, each fallen needle dwindles to plain mineral food. Thrifty pine. Where a boulder blocked this thin ravine, scree piled up and pine grows—root in shade, except at noon.

Stunted by cold, kinked by wind, this tree has no commercial value. America will not take this pine. It shall seek its own time.

Avalanche took the growing tip: snowpack five feet deep, the tip exposed and splintered away. Pine grows sideways.

Pine's failures remain: limbs thinned by shade. Sap goes up to the next lit branch. There are no mistakes.

Dressing in spring and undressing always, green pine sheds gold needles. I'm draped in an exotic ensemble of wool, cotton, steel eyelets, felt cap, and leather; pine bark stands dressed by sunlight, starlight, frost, rain.

This pine is one of many nameless wood souls on Strawberry Mountain, and is host to a few slow ants. I follow one from the root-maze of needles, up the twisted road of the trunk: stunted Eden of its kind.

Most thrifty angle for growth is a spiral bowed by snow: down, jut out, up, feint, twist, crack, bud.

At this altitude, pine wants little and has room. Nearest neighbor is stone underfoot, then lupine downslope at ten feet in a pocket of scree, then the wild roving grayjay rollicking downwind and perching but now and again. Pine simply entertains the wind. Contrast stone: wanting so little it never moves but to fall. Contrast lupine: wanting to be blue, soft, seasonal. Contrast grayjay: wanting so much it must flap and shout. Contrast my life.

In that shimmer downslope, at Hidden Lake, infant toads hunch poised at the warm seam between water and land. Pine does not seek marvels; marvels seek pine.

Pine has the vagabond heart of a hermit, the wild local character rooted to one place.

Branch out, slough off.

Pine has failed many times: twisted, split, shattered, beetle-bored through, scraped raw by ice, but not uprooted.

Wind has shaped the ridge-stone into waves. Pine clump shapes the wind. Pine forms and conforms.

Cambium is incredibly thin and busy: one perimeter of life. Yesterday, I slit open a trout and found the ant-hatch packed inside. I saw one spider harnessed to a two-fathom filament riding the vacant wind up over redstone ridge. I tasted the crimson throng of wild currant in their spiny thicket. All this time, pine stood blind.

Below, in a bump of meadow, penstemon is touched by an emerald hummingbird, buzzing from bloom to bloom. Only wind carries pollen for pine. Tap a twig in spring, and pine speaks gold pollen like smoke. What makes pine so good-humored?

Five-needle clump; five-finger fist.

That one word with so many articulations—that word wind makes through pine: I whisper Spanish, Old English, Latin, and the common names of trees. Nothing is old enough.

By starlit snow, wind gusting to eighty, chill factor absolute, winter pine still grows, but slower.

FIR had a poor name in the early days. Back East, pine was king, while fir was working citizen. The first Northwest lumber merchants, loading planks of Douglas fir onto the decks of schooners bound for San Francisco and south, called the wood Oregon pine. The tree is still called Oregon pine in most European languages, though it is technically a spruce. As a final confusion, its scientific name means "false hemlock": *Pseudotsuga.* To the Northwest innocent, it is simply the fir of the region. And it sold. When the California gold mines hungered, when San Francisco burned, the forests of the Northwest trembled. When the tallest known Douglas fir was felled in 1895, they summoned the sheriff to witness the crime and measure the corpse: four hundred and seventeen feet. Soon this wood was famous. It grew straight and clean for masts—the first branch a hundred feet up the stem in a thick stand. Fir tests stronger than steel, pound for pound, and it grew close grained in abundant old-growth groves. Dan Miles, an old-time logger, told me how to fall a nine-foot tree with a six-foot saw. It's a matter of clever notches and a mother's patience, he said. Once the tree was down, Dan and his brothers had to split that log with dynamite to fit it through the gang saw at the mill.

Back in Philadelphia, you can push a black button outside the glass house guarding the Liberty Bell, and a voice will tell you history—how that bell was cast and how it cracked and how the crack reached up to split the word "Liberty" while the bell tolled for Washington's birthday. It's an old sweet story. In Oregon, at the Western Forestry Center in Portland, a pillar of plastic and cement (pretending to be a fir tree six-foot through) has been wired for light and sound. When a visitor fingers the right black button, the tree speaks: "Welcome, welcome. . . ." And the story gets told of xylem carrying water up and phloem carrying sugar down: lights ripple within the trunk like the river of this life. "I must admit that I am just a talking tree," says the tree. "I can't even grow a single cell. All I can do is talk. Enjoy your visit, and remember me—the talking tree."

The actual voice saying "remember me" is the voice of a local newscaster. When it speaks, the pillar's voice has the local ring of authority that has pushed hard news at us for years. There is a story that the newscaster's daughter worked at the desk beside the talking tree. All day, all summer, visitors came in waves. As the crowds listened, gazed up along the long trunk, opened their silent mouths, again and again she heard her father say, in his trance of authority, "Let's pretend I'm a real tree . . . remember me."

The voice of an ancestor speaks rightly from a tree. At my home, the family tree is a literal sycamore. My grandmother gave it as a sapling: a stem crowned with a whorl of four branches for the four children. I am one. Now she has gone and it is giant shade, mossy with age, sprawling across the sky. Passing out the front door, we keep the custom of reaching out to touch its bark. It clatters in storms, and dumps mounds of dusty leaves. We stand against the trunk for photographs. ("There, that is Boppums in the background, the one dressed in lichen.") We climb or loll in her shade, rake her leaves, watch her roots knee up to buckle the walk. When we chop up a heavy limb that rubbed on the roof, my grandmother's fire warms us. Through the screen in December: remember me. And my deepest sense of home includes that soft rushing sound of wind through tall old fir trees.

"Can you remember your work as a logger?" I asked Milo,

an old bachelor living at eighty with his sister Cora. She was upstairs, sifting photographs to show me. I said to Milo, "Dan Miles tells me he filed saws on your crew—when was that, the twenties?"

First Milo gave me that customary silence of the old, that respectful hesitation. Then he said in a low voice, "When we worked big fir, I had a falling partner. He chopped left-handed, I chopped right, and that made us good partners. But you always have to brush out a trail to run. When the tree starts down, you're going to drop your saw and run. Before you springboard up and start the undercut, your two fallers always brush out a trail apiece. Get that tangle-vine maple and other trash out of your way. Tree goes here—you go this way, he goes that.

"Had our trails clear, got up ten foot past the butt-swell on springboards, threw coal-oil on the saw, and started that old misery whip back and forth. He was pulling hard that day, and I was bitching about it. 'Pull steady, dammit!' So he evens out. We got the undercut sawed, and chopped her out, then took a break for lunch. He wasn't talking. Trouble with his girl, maybe, trouble with his soul—I never did know. Silent break, and we went back at it silent. We were working a side canyon to ourselves. Real quiet, and that was odd. My partner usually talked along right with the saw. His talking muscle never got tired. But different that day.

"We climbed up to springboards again and started the backcut. Pretty soon we went out of view from each other—he swinging his board away as the saw went in, and he driving his own little wedge to keep the kerf open so the saw won't bind.

You saw a while, and tap that wedge, and the wood hinge between your undercut and backcut slims down to a couple fingers through, and then she goes. It's then you tap the wedge and it slips in loose, the backcut kerf starts to open, the tree-hinge starts talking, and you jump. We dropped the saw, and jumped down right, and I started running out along my trail without a backward look. You got to just go like hell from those old ones. Any kind of widowmaker trash can fall from the sky. But he didn't run. I could hear he didn't, because that big tree coming down was quiet at first. When I turned around, he stood looking at me, stood where the tree would drop.

"'Milo, you go on,' he says. Real quiet. There was that quiet before hell. 'Go on,' he says.

"A big limb gets him, tears him open and knocks him aside, and then the tree's down in its own blow of splinters and dust. I run around the stump to where he lies. I held him in my arms god-damn. He's all split open. I could see his heart, was working. He didn't talk. I didn't talk. Nobody came, and he didn't last. Yeah, my partner. Accident, they said. He stood there. 'Milo,' he says, 'you go on.'"

Milo looked me in the eye. Cara came back into the room. There was nothing more to say that day.

CEDAR rings like a bell when split, and a honey whisper rises from the riven shake. The plink of kindling, the clunk of fence rails struck from a log—dressing cedar boards is light, loving work. "Behold, thou art fair, my beloved," says the Song of Songs; "also our bed is green. The beams of our house are cedar, and our rafters of fir."

Makoto Imai, our teacher and Japanese builder of shrines, worked three hours before us to sharpen his tools before he hefted a rare beam of Port Orford cedar. "When you hold small tool," he said to us, "get it balanced like your hand. Your whole body need be very quiet." The room was quiet as he calligraphed the layout of a scarf-joint in the air before us with a tiny brush of crushed bamboo. We looked around. His tools lay before him on a simple plank—four saws, ten chisels, planes, a square, and the Japanese equivalent of a chalkline: a reel of silk thread with a turtle carved on it that sipped from the bowl of *sumi* ink. Behind him stretched years of exacting practice. He works for nothing sometimes, sleeping at the site of a slow-growing shrine. His tools showed more spirit than steel, more of karma than carpentry. Cedar does this to a listener.

Some read cedar for spirit, some read in it only the metaphor of value called money. So, cedar pirates abound. Moth doth not corrupt, rain doth not soften cedar. Clear heartwood redcedar asks a fair price, and all along the Pacific beach after each storm the big silver driftlogs have been tasted by a beachcomber's axe. A cedar pirate chips wood and sips the wind. If the smell is cedar, he'll be back with a truck, a chainsaw, and a winch. A good western redcedar log can lie damp in the Northwest woods for generations and still prove sound to the saws of the shingle-mill. A flatbed truck stacked high with fresh-cut bundles of cedar shingles will leave a trail of scent half a mile long. Following such a load as I spin down the freeway, I pop open the wind-wing and drink deep: sweet intoxication. The air in Pharaoh's tomb was magic, but cedar mixed with wind is food.

For the Kwakiutl, Nootka, Haida, Bella Bella, and other people of the Northwest coast, cedar bark and wood made rain-proof hat, tasseled cape, box for the dead, housepost face, tall tree carved to the masks of totem, rope to tether whales. When they paddled long cedar canoes boiling upriver, they pulled the wide cedar planks of their homes in rafts. In a Chinook story, when Coyote was trapped in a hollow cedar tree, he had to tear himself apart and slip out bone by bone through a woodpecker hole. But a raven made off with his eyes. Then Coyote tricked an old woman blind to steal back sight. He went off with her eyes, and she with a pair of wild rose leaves. But the story is not about Coyote, or the snail that old woman became, feeling her way along the ground forever. The story is about cedar. Coyote tried to be the spirit of a tree, and failed. Cedar held the life.

"Life is for doing things slow," Makoto said, "like trees." We learned much from this man, because he was humble, articulate as the figure in wood itself. He taught us with demon-strative movements more like dance than knowledge, and with a level gaze. His few words only confirmed what his working showed. "Learning with the body—slow, strong," he said at one point, as he paused between chisel strokes. "Learning with the head—fast, easy to forget." The long shaving fell away hesitant as lace from his blade. When others edged forward to touch the scarf-joint he had made, I bent to lift the shaving and hold it to my face, like a message I had inherited, breathing in deep.

Makoto wished his dovetail joint, his tenon fit to be tight as the integral growth of wood. He worked with a tree's patience. "In sharpening, in joinery," he said, "you must use listening sound, trying to be concentrate. Must be quiet in the shop when you sharpen—talk, machine, it will not work." He chose the tree of life: "If you are working for money, use maybe marking gauge; for yourself, a bamboo brush, *sumi* ink. That is the pleasure for your whole body, making a beautiful thing."

YEW is a magic stick. When I was twelve, I found it lost in the barn. My nine cousins swung from the rope to perish in hay so deep it muffled their laughter, rising as they did to play Kansas kamikaze again. From above, I watched them die and rise, in the freedom of the tribe of nine. I was one of four—expendable, yes, but not to the power of nine. And I was from Oregon: for all the glory of the barn, of summer Kansas, a little homesick.

Hid among the cluttered steamer trunks and Midwest history—letters from the Civil War, and horse gear mice inhabited—I found the magic stick: a short yew bow without a string. It was just my height, with a red heartwood belly and a perfectly thin sapwood back. There was a leather handle, and in dim dusty light my fingers followed the notches at the ends so neatly grooved with a rat-tail file—the nocks where a string should fit. I tested it against my knee. The bow was stiff, its limbs tapering hardly at all.

The real magic of the thing was not its strength, but its blemish. A few inches from one end, the wood took a sharp kink where the maker had followed the grain faithfully around a knot in the original tree. A lesser hand would have taken a saw to the blank, and cut straight through, losing strength for symmetry. My fingers curled around that kink. Someone understood the true crippled world could be stronger than plain beauty. Some-one had followed the grain.

Someone was calling the nine, and they called for me. I came down the long ladder with the bow through my belt. "Oh, that," said the nine, "that bow." I was the finder. I felt I had a claim.

Inside the big house, in the swirl for a place at the sink to wash, my father said, "Let me see that bow." In his hands it was real, and the big glass of the window shimmered in danger from the invisible arrow he pulled. His face tightened into the scowl for aim, and the nine stood back at bay, Uncle Bob and Mar saying, "Bill, your bow."

It was his bow. He had cleft a billet from a bolt of Oregon yew, shaved it down with shards of glass, following the grain past that true kink, spliced the original linen bowstring, and sent this gift to the Kansas cousins. When lives were shorter, people had time for such work. The bow lasted with the tribe the life of one string, and when the mice got that, the bow moved upstairs into the barn of history.

I felt that bow was a wood soul far from home. Shouldn't wood and I live where we began? The nine were generous. Driving west, in the back seat I held it: homeward cousin, Oregon yew.

What makes yew the living talisman of change? What makes it spry for bows and tuneful for the backs of lutes? Some-thing in its tight red grain older than religion makes it right for killing and for music. Up the McKenzie River, just before the road from Sweet Home joins the highway for Sisters, yew trees huddle in a grove, north upslope. I always seem to get there just at dark, and snow lights the ground where I stand among them. The branches turn abruptly back on themselves like the rune named *yew,* the rune for death. I want to ask their twisted forms "Does it hurt so much, coming out of the ground?" I lean on a trunk. The pitchy berries are dull red, the flat needles still. Then starlight.

Pascal said a strange thing: the sole cause of human unhappiness is our inability to remain quietly at home in our rooms. In a fist of working forest duff are more small lives than the human population of Earth: in secret, a busy power of being. Eden is there, compact. Heaven for a yew tree lies below. Is this why yew stands bent but cheerful? "Our songs are short," said the Papago woman, "because we understand so much." Yew stays home, grows slow, lives long: guest most faithful to this ground.

ANY TABLE of virgin fir, any maple chair, any oak floor is a bundle of stories. At a lull in the conversation, move your napkin aside. There are centuries under one hand's span, and the timbre of a long, spirited life for the rap of a knuckle. Woodworkers sometimes hear it—the sweetest yelp of the violin before they brush on the varnish of maturity. There was a man who made rifle stocks of curly maple. His son made skiffs of Sitka spruce. Both gave up their ways, and sold their wood to my friend, who makes violins: spruce for the bellies, maple for the backs, with ebony fingerboards. So it has always been done. Tree of life, teach us to give up war and distance for the plain, local thrill of this music: pine, fir, cedar, yew.

THE GREAT DEPRESSION AS HEROIC AGE

HEARTBEAT takes me forward, stories take me back. Waking on the midnight train, or wakeful in my bed at home, in orbit memory I hurtle past the houses where my people grew. I ramble the vagabond circuit, the foggy geography of time, and glance through windows lit by a pincushion on a table, a book in hand. In this Kansas house my father will live. At this Nebraska farm my mother will arise. Tornado wants them dead. Fear wants them sad. I batter with the moth on screen doors, sipping a rusty fragrance, wanting in. My wings dissolve, I wake. I travel locally. In Oregon back home, when we gather for tea, I listen hard. In stories from the Great Depression and the ribbons of experience it sent outward, my kin live simply. By their telling, hard times trained them to be happy. Their hardship stories work on me. Before dawn, alone at my desk, I try to sift it all, to give it all a shape. On this computer screen, my words spin green from light. How shall I live?

One winter day on the bus bound east through central Oregon, just as we dropped over the rim to the reservation at Warm Springs, I glanced across the aisle at a Wasco boy. He cradled a book that devotion had worn to tatters: *The Incredible Magic of the American Indian.* Late sunlight struck the page and lit his face, his eyes that hunted as he read. One seat back, in the hands of a ski bum about the same age, I saw Kerouac's *On the Road.* He traveled the kinked road twice: once by body, once by mind. The bus geared down. Outside, the steep sage hills tapered into darkness. I put my hand to the heart-pocket of my coat, where I had tucked away a tiny notebook to write down what I heard and saw and remembered—my own chosen stories of magic and departure. Traveling alone, each of us carried a book as medicine bundle, as survival kit of stories, as possible sack of belief and remedy to help us through the world.

Late that night, when I arrived in Burns, I learned my shirts and socks and sleeping bag had all caught the wrong bus in Bend. Surely now they traveled toward Los Angeles. The woman at the station counter, sleepy and ready to close, would put a tracer on my pack, she said, in the morning. Her hand on the counter flicked open, then slowly folded shut to show her regret and her fatigue. Beside her hand, in a rusted coffee can, a spindly tomato vine still grew—her pet and a February miracle. Marooned in Burns, I would grow beyond my custom, too.

I turned away, starting off for the all-night Elkhorn Cafe. Outside, wind pumped snow and newspapers along the street. When the station lights had flickered out, the stars shone bold.

When you lose everything, what do you lose, and what do you keep? When you move with short notice, what do you take along? That night in Burns, I thought of the people of Sugar City, Idaho, the people told by bullhorn the dam had given way and they had minutes to abandon their homes and scramble for high ground. One man grabbed his electric razor and ran. A woman gathered only her Hümmels with one loving sweep of her arms, and lurched away. The last man out just had time to snatch his cowboy hat before clambering into his nephew's wading pool and spinning away on the flood down Main Street. Before the water went down, it erased the town with a smear of mud, but everyone had a story.

I had to leave like that, and now I travel, an exile at a distance of thirty years from childhood. I carry stories from the old country, the point of origin, the central decade of the family's hard times. The Great Depression of the thirties makes our heroic age, our *Iliad*, our *Odyssey*, our trickster Coyote's time before the world was changed. I travel by bus, by foot, by dark, with a heart-pocket bundle of stories that light the road.

BY HABIT I carry this notebook in my pocket, and travel as professional eavesdropper, because of the training I bring from home. When I played student there, my mother had a beautiful listening ear for our stories, and my father had a teacher's fine trick that made us feel part of something big. When one of the four wild kids would mention a fugitive thought, an idea in infancy, no matter how small, my mother would draw us out for more, or my father would stop the talk to savor what we had said. Often, they would match our saying to a line from literature or a story from the family lore. The literature flavored our lives then, but the stories stuck for good.

"Daddy, when I held the bow and arrows this time, I thought how Bobbie Elliot can hit a baseball better, but I know how to shoot."

"You know," my father would say, "Milton had the same idea." He would reel out a grand, soothing passage then from *Paradise Lost,* a stretch of line from Shakespeare, a chanted reverie from Wordsworth, from George Eliot, Willa Cather, Thomas Mann. He would knot our feeble syllables to the cadences of the great. The exact words of the poetry did not stay with me, but the feeling of being companion to Shakespeare struck like a bell in my heart. Child, parent, and saint of the language joined as fellow pilgrims on one road.

It happened the same with family stories, but I remember the stories. In the teaching episodes from my parents' memories, customs from Kansas and Nebraska where they grew might get linked to any detail from our lives. Packed in my parents' granary minds, stories sprang from seed. When we made small complaints, our whine could sprout a story from that golden void.

"My milkshake's all plugged up. I need a bigger straw!"

"In *Kansas,*" my father would answer, as if citing scripture, "my father would take us in the Model T to a wheatfield at the edge of town, and we'd each cut a real straw the mowing machine had left. Then at home in the evening, my mother would make strawberry milkshake—strawberry jam dropped in a quart of milk and shaken. Sure the seeds got stuck in the wheatstraw. That just slowed us down enough to taste it."

Maybe the way he told it made our lives taste pale. Every Nebraska day and every Kansas story had a flavor like that. Exotic black cars lived there, and mysterious fathers taking kids out for a spin. A wheatfield bristled close to home, and beyond it, we knew, ran Cow Creek, and monster catfish, and nights of shenanigans trapping, tramping about, camping out, being alone. You could sip on a real wheatstraw, not this plastic. You could stand in that trim kitchen Ruby brightened, not this drive-in blacktop spotted with gum.

My father's father, Earl, traveled for the power company, taking great sweeps to the southwest from Hutchinson, from El Dorado, from Liberal. He dropped the boys off one time near Capulin Mountain in New Mexico.

"I'll be back through in ten days," he said. "Can you make it north by then to Cottonwood Canyon? I think so, too. So long."

The boys traveled cross-country, slept in caves, and licked flat pools after rain. They shot quail, rabbits, and doves with a deadeye twenty-two. They could strike a match with that gun, my father said, if they ever had to. One day they ate only a robin, sharing it wing by wing over the fire. Once at a ranch, they traded the story of their quest for a meal. They met a plowman in a dry canyon, and he took them home for stories and peaches dried in the sun. In ten days, sixty miles north from their starting place, Earl met them. He had given them a test and freedom.

"Did you face danger then, wandering around like that?" I asked my father on his birthday once.

"The world was all attached," he said. "If only we could get lost." As always, the story sent an invitation to us.

In the thirties, poverty gave our people a test and freedom. My father took a string of difficult jobs, and a few dangerous ones—fighting fire at the oil refinery, and holding the steel shaft of a star-drill with his hands for a clumsy roustabout to drive and drive with the sledge flashing over his head. Tornadoes came through on a binge. The Klan ran rife. Diphtheria struck. When his sister lay near death, my father burst into the room, boisterous from play.

"Is she dead yet?" he shouted. She lived, but his bright shout spun from the same family pluck that carried her through. That pluck made the heroic time. Did our small troubles deserve the name?

"Don't pay any attention," my father said to our blackberry scratches or sidewalk bruises. When we whined over small defeats, my father came back with a Kansas joke.

"They asked the boy, 'Are you full yet, son?'

" 'No,' he says, 'I'm not full. I'm just down to where it don't taste good no more.' "

FROM NEBRASKA, the story-testament from Brethren farmers on my mother's side speaks most of change. The Frantz family must have webbed the whole southern quilt of Nebraska. They kept moving, preaching, homesteading around. In the books that come down from that time, the names on the flyleaves read the same, but the places keep hopping about. They farmed or studied or took the interim pastorate in Illinois, then Nebraska, then Wyoming, then Nebraska again, Kansas, Colorado, California, Pennsylvania, and Heaven. For me, these stories winnow down from my mother, Dorothy Hope; from her older sister, Helen; and from their mother, Lottie, the grandmother my brother named forever "Boppums."

The Bible held the public secrets of those days. The palm-sized New Testament that belonged to child-Lottie burrows into my hand, soft as a favored doll worn ragged with affection. Back home in Oregon, I take it up this week to learn the code I saw painted on a car, a moss-green Dodge slung low. The driver before me at the stoplight, a prim and vintage woman, had drawn this message fine as embroidery gold on the black ground of her smashed rear bumper: "Jesus on Reagan—Matt. 23:14." In my notebook, I took that down. At my home desk, I open to that verse: "Woe onto you, scribes and Pharisees, hypocrites! for ye devour widows' houses, and for a pretense make long prayer: therefore ye shall receive the greater damnation." The Bible spoke her mind.

The brown spine of that book lingers threadbare. The cover falls open easy as a hand releasing prayer. But if that book held the public secrets, another held Boppums' own. We found it in her drawer—a slim, brown notebook locked shut with melted wax and a ribbon. Above the wax, writ faint in her black scrawl, this line: "Sealed till Finished." No one would read it until she died.

Looking back by orbit memory, which window shall I trust above all? I have an account of my grandparents' wedding from the Beatrice, Nebraska, *Semi-Weekly* for June 17, 1902:

A little before 7 o'clock about fifty guests assembled in the
parlors to witness the ceremony. Promptly at 7 amid the strains
of the wedding march, rendered by Miss Daisy Wardlaw of
Pickrell, the bride and groom entered the parlor and took their
places under a beautiful portiere of green vines and roses. They
were preceded by little Evelyn Miller, who acted her part well
as flower girl, strewing roses before them.

The news account tells it sweetly, but has no heart. When
Boppums died, we cut the ribbon on her book, "Sealed till
Finished." Under the ribbon, she had written, "The New Life
of Lottie." The new life bloomed there, now so old it lived in
us. The cover had been closed so long, it held shut, reluctant
to bend away from these first words:

> This then is to be the day of days. How I shall feel when
> today is over and I am no longer my mother's baby but—
> Harry's wife. Wonderful words. It is to be a full day for a
> hundred things or two must be done—

At nineteen years, Lottie wrote that much, then went down to
do her hundred chores in a daze—to hang the rope of green-
ery, arrange the oranges in their bowl, slip down to the cellar
to see to the fixings for supper, run to the gate to meet her
Harrison, and scramble through all the small emergencies of
change. When the day had finished, darkened, she came back to
her book and wrote all down, somewhere later that night. A few
hours launched on her new life, already she looked back. The
future tense had changed.

> Then Sadie motioned us to come, and I taking the strong arm
> that I was hereafter to lean upon walked slowly through the
> crowded room into the parlor keeping time to the beautiful
> music. Then Aaron stood before us; I can just feel again like
> I did at that moment.

Thus the New Life's first day ends. Harrison, the groom, lived devout, a farmer, carpenter, preacher, yet I have never heard or read his words. The diary of Lottie, the new life of this quiet woman half my age, stands for all. After her description of the wedding day—whether for joy, terror, confusion—the next stretch of pages in the book and six months of her life run blank. Did she mean to come back someday and fill this blank? Someday, with greater wisdom, she might understand such changes that first darkness brought. I know they lived with her mother then. For a time, one story says, they inhabited the barn, stacking sweet bales of alfalfa hay for walls, tables, chairs, and bed. In a photograph, their wedding gifts rise up in a great mound of crockery, linens, and glassware. Her book says nothing of these.

After this twenty-five page gap, the next entry in her book names January 1, 1903, and the tone has changed: "Thursday morning this is and we must pack. Thursday evening this is and we have packed." Again, she writes from both ends of a day, but she has entered the rush of straight chore, whim, custom, and hope of the world. That rush includes Harrison selling the farm, a neighbor killing himself with fire, meetings for prayer and hymn, depression, moonlight, comfort, and toil.

"Harrison built our house today," Boppums reports from their Wyoming homestead. The next day, "Harrison sawed a hole for a window in the wall." Then, after a storm, "Harrison propped the house with a pole to keep it standing through the night." They went broke, won back their stake, and crossed the Mojave west to the Promised Land. In the thirties once, at their little college in La Verne, California, the faculty voted to go all year without salary to save the college from ruin. This would only take a slight acceleration in their habits of thrift and cooperation. Somehow, they made it through. Somehow, even in that year, they still gave a meal whenever a tramp knocked. Not content with sufficiency, Boppums joined the weekly Ladies' Aid Society to piece and quilt coverlets to give away for charity. Like her stories after her time, somewhere now those quilts warm others, strangers, travelers.

In the first years, the traveling years, Boppums found her own way by stories. With child a third time, she followed a particular belief to my mother's making. Someone told her she must spend each day of her pregnancy looking on beautiful things. Flowers, a pleasing shadow on the lawn, sunset, the moon over water—these the child within would need. Each evening, Boppums would put down her work and stand on the porch to help the colors of the sky nourish her child. She put the secrets of new life in her sealed book, and the secrets of beauty in her children.

At the end of their life together, Harrison and Lottie went back to live among the Amish of Lancaster County, Pennsylvania. A kindly woman took them in for years there. They reaped what they had sown, the sweet hospitality of the heroic age.

At my desk, I put down the Bible, take up her diary with the broken seal, and ask myself, what should I quilt and hide, and when will I finish? In this city, what secrets, what new life should I now tuck away, so children may break the seal, and witness nourishing ways?

BOPPUMS KEEPS a little room upstairs in my head to do her

ironing and storytelling, to mend and recite, to suffer horizontal her final illness, and then to stand up breathless the morning of her wedding when Harrison came riding on his horse, bent down at the gate, and kissed her on the mouth in front of everyone. In her room, glass curtains billow inward. The door swings open, lit by lilac and flat sunlight, then by kerosene. Threadbare travelers of grace tap at the door, drift through the house, leave their names in the Bible, and pass on. Alone, she looks up from the hem she stitches to watch a moth batter the lamp. Then she looks down at me, drawn up by light through the small wick hatch to stand at her knee.

"Tell about the fishermen," I say, "and the storm."

"Nebraska?" she mumbles. The straight pins between her lips wiggle and gleam.

"Yes, Nebraska, please." My elbows rest on her knees. The apron, safety-pinned to her bosom, hangs up a blue meadow busy with pockets. Here her thimble clatters like a little bell, and there her scissors twinkle and snip. Between finger and thumb, she spreads the pins from her mouth like a tiny fan. Her hymn-voice trembles. Pins to the cushion, story to me.

"One time, Kimney-pie, we all went out to the lake—threshing done, the barn full. The men took up their net and waded in. August, so the water ran mild. The Lord stood by us. They made a great catch of fishes, and everyone, even the children, stepped into the water to help them haul in that net. We had cottonwood fires to prepare the fish. Then men laid their black coats down over bundles of straw, and women spread a white cloth on the earth. Can you imagine—a white cloth, and everything washed by hand? We broke open the bread, and read from the Book. We prayed, we ate, we talked of the year. But as we sang, a great storm came up. I remember the lake rolling gray, and thunder. I can see lighting pricking the horizon like that."

She pricks the back of her hand with the silver needle, red thread trailing.

"The men cried out. 'Aaron, does lightning fall on your house there? And there, Miley, yours?' But the storm passed over us. No tornado then, no blaze. We calmed the horses. The moon rose to show us our way home."

In my head then, Boppums bends down. She sews and hums. Her story ends, but not the sewing. Not ever.

Once, when I came home from college, I learned that story had never happened. No lake, no black coats, they said. At least no one could remember it. Did I confuse the time Jesus called the fishermen from the Sea of Galilee? Did I stitch the New Testament story to a Nebraska storm? The saints of the family fit the Bible better than they fit my first world of the 1950s. In my small head, it seems, the heroic age had snatched a story from Bible culture and pinned it to the family lore.

After Boppums died, when I lay down for sleep one night, in the fragile trance between light and defeat an odd sentence spoke to me: "If my grandmother were alive today, she would be ten feet tall." I snapped back wakeful, wondering. Surely logic pulled that sentence out. Once I stood only tall enough to climb her lap, and listen to stories. Now that I am grown, she stands above me like ripe corn or moon, heroic goddess of age.

THE FAMILY STORIES took on starch when I first came across Depression photographs by Walker Evans. In his images of poverty's troubling elegance, I got smuggled back alive, and saw the vague evening glow of heartland stories brightened to noon. Taken by daylight, his photographs stare nevertheless like lit night windows, and I stare back. I see through them to hidden summer, to the Great Depression where a grand, spare order of hard sunlight blooms, a secret flavor of cool interiors. In that tranquility, the human face becomes a hieroglyph for persistence. A father feeds his children by the sheer mule-pull of his face. A mother stares flat at the camera, as if it has said to her what no one ever said: "Will you rest a moment, please?" The plainest object shudders in a sacramental glow: table, broom, churn, bowl, bed. By foglight, the pool hall façade flexes its cathedral splendor. In the sanctuary, Sabbath light on the Sunday-school organ unfurls a tool for justice. In a farmer's room, the wicker chair mended with wire stands as a throne sufficient for an afternoon of eternity.

What his camera loved, I love. Through these windows, I stand in attendance there. I wait upon my people. Evans and his companion of rumpled inspiration, James Agee, drove south to Alabama in July of 1936. What Agee called "the object of our traveling" was to form "an independent inquiry into certain normal predicaments of human divinity." Their traveling brought them to three families in the hills, and to the making of the book *Let Us Now Praise Famous Men*. That book delves by the blade of light and the tools of dreaming deep into the local habits of day and night, toil and praise. Few have read Agee's night-writ prose, but every family must write such a book. By such chapters, every family lives: "A Country Letter," "Money," "Shelter," "Clothing," "Education," "Work."

What they did by traveling, we do by memory. We travel back by stories, forward by the hope those stories teach. We center our account where Evans and Agee set out, the heart of the thirties. What they did by giving order to a book, chapter by chapter, we do by telling troubles in the rich, thankful light of the voice. We make stories of stories by changing them. Stories from other times get pruned away from chronology and grafted onto that hard decade's stump. When Boppums hungered and wrote her Wyoming homestead diary in 1915, she rehearsed a part for our heroic age. When my own baby bottle froze solid in 1951, but I survived beside it on the back seat of the family Dodge hurled across Iowa, that story fit backward into the decade of light. We lived in a Quonset of tin. Have we done better since? At the age of eight, I tried to convince my parents we could buy an abandoned chickenhouse, trim away the blackberry vines, build a wood floor on the earth, and all move in. That house wrote my greatest dream.

History names "The Great Crash of 1929," and history names "The Great Depression," as if only money could give backbone to a mood, and the human spirit must lie sickened by the slack thermometer of the price index. It may have seemed so then, but family stories have it otherwise. Somehow, bitterness, if it lived then, died later. By family stories, our spirits rose up in those days and boldly walked the Earth.

What made us bold, in stories? What made us up and about when others were down and out, according to the news? For one thing, families simply do not follow the same chronology as history. The growth of calendar years, the summerwood rings in a tree, the concentric rim on the flat scales of salmon—all play out sequential and exact. Families never do.

One night, across the mountains from home, we sat by candlelight with Mrs. Bell, a family friend. We launched our cabin through the night with stories. We told Kansas. We told Iowa. We told chickenhouse. When her turn came, she set the full spread of her family tree beside the little sapling of American history.

"Take my grandfather," she said, sipping red wine. "He was alive when George Washington was President. Think not? Hah! I know it's hard to believe." The fire rattled and the wind bent low. How many winters could fill a man's life? You had to do more than die to fit the pantheon.

"You see," she said, "he was born in 1796, grew up on the family's New Jersey farm, but he was not in haste to marry. His parents died, he ran the place alone. The Civil War came, and the story says Grandpa was working his hayfield when two blue soldiers came riding by, whipping their horses to foam and shouting the alarm.

" 'Lincoln dead—shot dead by assassin!'

" 'Fine!' shouted Grandpa back. 'About time someone got the old buzzard!' And he swung his scythe with happy spite. Oh, he was an odd one. But with the War done then, and Grandpa ripened to seventy, he courted and won a young lass of twenty-three. She planned, no doubt, to inherit his farm and live on past his timely end. Not so. She bore three children to him—my father the third—and then she died."

Mrs. Bell sipped again. Out across the meadow, a coyote lingered howling on a word, and soon others joined in all along the creek. In her story, the middle of the nineteenth century seemed closer than the coyote's frosty message. Abe nudged us. George gave us his firm grin. Our candles burned low.

"Well," she said, "Grandpa tyrannized the children four years past his hundred, before they laid him under the hill. Father was fifty when he married, in 1920, and that puts me here before your very eyes, never mind how old."

Her face startled the candlelight, bold as wine. She sipped. We sat back marveling. Statistics proved her story probable. How do things go? In our simple daze of wine and midnight, the family table between us billowed wide as a century, and contracted to a coffin pod. Story by story, the lips of Mrs. Bell made the proud scroll of the calendar dwindle away.

Stories work to make us more than citizens. A story does to history what a nickname does to a friend. Nothing can stand quite so proud without constantly proving its worth. "What are Indians used for?" my brother asked when small. My parents wrote that down in the family notebook called "Lost Words," but later changed to "Voices Remembered." Then, curiosity spoke. Later, he studied anthropology. He tried to learn why the question was wrong and true. Saved stories make us flexible. A good story makes a tool handy as that famous device patented in 1862, the "Improvement in combined house, bridge, boat, and wagon body." We inhabit, cross over, drift away, and haul stories home. In the Walker Evans photograph of the sweat, sorrow, and tenacity of the Gudger family, August 1936, light bit silver black and saved them for eternity. In our stories, conviction bites my soul.

ON A HOT AUGUST day in a strange town, I reached back for
the strength of family ways. I reached back for the decade that
brought balance to the world—the balanced trade of shriveled
possession for a swell in the power of being. When I approached
an apartment building, stern matriarch of brick between Main
and Arthur streets in Pocatello, Idaho, I saw it all by the heroic
flame that lit so many family travels: to move, find, celebrate.
The lettering above the door shone gold on black, but dark gold
burnished with decay, mottled by the sun: THE FARGO. The
steps to the heavy glass door took a grand, chipped sweep, and
the knob polished my hand green with brass. Then the long carpeted hush of the hall unreeled my shadow like a rope, each
door a varnished lid for the particular joys and desperations of
one life.

Halfway down the hall the wide stairs rose, the carpeted
spiral of the stairs a four-sided cage of dark wood climbing into
the past. My hand on the banister touched the spot where
everyone, living and dead, had gripped this silk wood for the
first heave upward. Even the young men courting, taking the
climb three steps at a time then skipping back down, grabbed
here. And the railroad pensioners, the old women with their
laundry duffel, tramps looking for a carpeted sleep in the hall
took their hold on the same palm-sized bump of mahogany.
Down from the skylight, a pillar of sunlight stood cool with dust.

For me, that three-story box of stairs held the holy hush
and honest age of the thirties. I climbed that chamber of human
time, surging upward in the wing-harness of family myth. I
climbed counterclockwise, in the spiral gyre not of progress but
of sloughing off, of shucking prosperity for happiness. In such

a place, Utopia would rise up, a neighborhood among us: the kindly, jabbering Toombs sisters in 101; Rex the railroad handyman always on the prowl to help; and the man everyone called Old Holy Socks camped in the cellar.

That first day, on the landing of the second floor, where the purple weave of the carpet frayed out brown, I knew where to step. Other travelers had left a path that showed in each bald palm of carpet, under the pillar of sun and the candlelight glow of small bulbs. I put my feet down where they were meant to go, where I could feel the real floor not softened by plush, and hear the crack and flex of oak flooring that came by rail. I held the key Doris Garner, the manager in apartment A, had given. I let my eyes go dim from focus, and shuffled down the corridor toward the door of 202. The key in my hand shot a hot blue spark into the lock, and I slipped inside.

How can I see that apartment now? The bright shock of our daughter's subsequent birth has rinsed any dingy shadow from the room. Old couch sags comforting in mind. The skeleton bed that greeted me then has dressed since in my wife's early labor, the counting breath by breath through pain to joy. A quilt softened by a thousand nights of our life now covers every rusted squeak of my first touch. Didn't that dust-pocked and cracked window speak only of sunlight dazzle then?

Outside, in the heavy glint of August, my wife wilted in the car. We had come to Idaho to take a one-year job and have a child. We traveled poor, but knit by lore. Story by story I had been schooled for this. In the thirties, hadn't my father dressed in harness and pulled a plow for ten cents an hour? Hadn't my mother traveled in her Sabbath best to trade hymns for meals? They had met and said simply, "Shouldn't it always be this way?"

That night, from the high, cracked windows of The Fargo, we could see the red glitter of the Dead Horse Saloon, and the neon wagon wheel on the Yellowstone Hotel, where rumor said the manager moved from room to room, using them up, leaving them locked and cluttered like our nation moving through the decades. Slipping out for work before first light, I stepped carefully around sleeping drunks stretched warm on the carpet of the hall. After November, I didn't drive our buried car for three straight months of snow, but walked everywhere—past the smoky Harlem Club, the cemetery filled with Japanese names, the Bannock County historical shrine of local knickknacks. Coal dust billowed out from empty cradle-cars. I cut across the rail-yard to haunt the Old Timers' Cafe like a kid loose in the tool-shop of history.

In a winter of Pocatello life, I saw the ways familiar to me from family stories out of another time. An Idaho bumper-sticker has it that "Idaho is what America was." I saw this in the Pocatello custom of the underground house. By this custom, a family will scrape together the money to start building, get the hole dug by June and the basement in, lay down the floor for the actual house, cover the floor with tarpaper, and batten down for a first winter. Only an antenna shows above ground for the television, and a stovepipe, and a boxed little set of stairs sprouting from the earth like a turret with roof, door, and hand-painted house number. After a few winters, the antenna turns rusty, and they have mopped down tar to make the roof last. The family has decided to quit building toward respectability, and call her good. They all live snug and quiet in the earth. Out the slit windows at ground level, you can recognize visitors by watching their shoes come up along the path.

Up on the bench of sage-ground west from town a vacant house shows another way to wrestle with thrift and necessity. There the log cabin of telephone poles holds a lid of earth, a pelt of blond grass swaying. Whoever left this place, left in a hurry. Several dozen television sets frost the yard in a wizardry of disrepair. A hole in the door once let the cat slip through, with a flap of red carpet nailed in place to keep out wind. Inside, the stove looms out of all proportion to the size of the room—they kept it warm. Religious literature covers the floor, and self-help guitar lessons, farm journals, amateur electronics digests. That first day I visited, I picked up one book in the fading snow-light of evening: *New Heaven and New Earth*. In the closet, a blue wool coat hung like new.

One cold night, at the west edge of town, my moon-tailored wife and I climbed the two hundred and seven concrete steps to the old community dance floor—a half-acre of packed earth surrounded by sage. To the west, not a single house-light burned, clear to Kingport Mountain. East, we looked back down at Pocatello glorying in her lit streets, the throb of her trains, the haste of cars on Main, a shout and an answer now and again. In two days, our daughter was due and the world would change.

"Hold me. Hold me now and dance by starlight."

AFTER IDAHO, back home in Oregon, I heard my mother and her sister laughing in the other room, laughing so they couldn't stop. They had found a magazine Boppums had saved from the first years of her marriage, and in it an article on how to keep your family small.

"Take your husband to a film," my mother read aloud, "or to the theater. This will take his mind off you." And then laughter, joyful laughter of the survivors—those of us who live to laugh because of our ancestors' lucky foolishness. Hard family stories thrust into my heart this one unspoken fact: children, oh children, our strange ways result in you.

And so it goes. Two of my friends use their expensive college educations to make pottery and have twins and live in the oldest house and be poor. They walk everywhere, swinging through the neighborhood with that long-distance tramp's easy gaze on our opulence. They scrounge and mend, rather than buy and install. They ramble among us lean, magnets for sympathy. They furnish their house with a fraction of what their neighbors throw away. The roof shingles curl, and the walls craze with cracked paint. The small yard shows puritan grass clipped flat, and a lush garden where cucumbers flourish, and corn, tomatoes, butterflies.

They live some desperate days, and take tough jobs for small pay. They inherit a conscience from their parents, and are strong. By this conscience, they have traded away security for freedom. They try to live right. By night, their curtains show the soft light of kerosene.

"Why do they do this?" the husband's father asks his friends. "They live in voluntary poverty. They could do better if they wished." Yet I know that father taught them to live this way. When he tells about his own first car, when he brags how he reached out the window in the rain to jerk a cotton string to make the wipers flail, his voice takes a jump of laughter that flattens over the decades of prosperity. He taught them too well, as my parents taught me, that hard times make good stories, and good stories make rich lives.

Oklahoma taught Woody Guthrie this, and Guthrie taught Bob Dylan this, and Dylan taught my generation this. When I heard "Blowin' in the Wind" tamed to muzak at the shopping mall, I felt a rage for truer ways: not a loudspeaker, but the honest rasp of a familiar voice. Not a good job, but good work, important work—the kind you take when what they call "recession" pinches off the end of a national binge. How many lives of quiet desperation will it take till we know this? The answer, my friends, makes our life work.

When the Tsimshian dancers of the Northwest coast lowered their masked faces and came to rest, they would end their singing, and speak by custom to those who watched.

"You do not see us dancing today—you see your ancestors dancing today. And now you will wear their stories. You will wear their stories that never grow old."

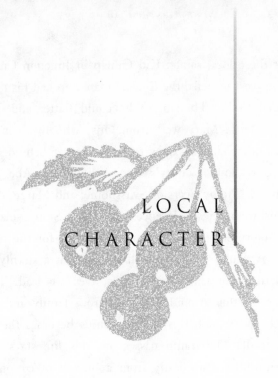

LOCAL CHARACTER

GYPSY SLIM taught me why each town's outcast eccentric is its patron saint. Until he disappeared, Slim camped by the downtown library in Portland. His plastic tarp stretched between two shopping carts and the stone bench carved with the name of that rebel from the Enlightenment, Laurence Sterne. When citizens would clip along past him, haughty with respectability, Gypsy Slim would jive them with an easy line of talk, until he had them stalled long enough for a real earful: "I don't care if it's family, friend, house, job, creed, ethnic group, country, institution, or sex—they *all* try to stifle what *you* can be." Then his saxophone would wrangle their hearts for yes or no.

In every Oregon town where I live or camp, I hear stories

about these local saints: Kid Gilnap in Junction City, with his jingling vest of bells; the Eugene man who had his name legally changed to Pro Human, so he could flatter and counsel the young; Bottle Mary west from Otis, who lived on returnable bottles other citizens knew to leave for her behind a particular stump; Wallowa County's own Acy Deucy; Abe Johnson of Redmond; Tubby Beers of Swisshome; and Marge, the gatherer of mushrooms near Florence. As Gypsy Slim explained, these most unorthodox lives become a standard for the rest of us— not a particular way for us all to live, but a sternly individual standard to measure the various lives we lead. The hermit belongs to this ground. Separate from family and career and church and school, this shabby genius becomes the life of the place itself. The tramp passes on; this life stays. A tattered American flag flaps lazily from a branch of cottonwood near Celilo. When the eastbound freight thunders past, a gray hand flickers from the shadows to wave.

The saint dwells alone in a house or camp that defies the surface formalities of the town. Being alone, she or he is uniquely visible to the community, and uniquely free to live out some kind of wishing we cannot. Sweet paradox: the local character is independent of the codes we live by, and by this independence is free to honor some deeper code or devotion that we—in our upright ways—believe but cannot express. This may be a devotion to a submerged traditional culture, to the past, to the vulnerable creatures of the natural world, or to the plain dignity of the slow mind.

FRIENDS TOLD ME to watch for Acy Deucy, his big black hat

sagging over his shoulders, as he walked toward Wallowa from his cabin twenty miles out. He'd come slouching along the country road each Saturday afternoon, with a local river's easy tread. And we traded stories at his expense—about the summer shack where he lived desperate summer and winter high on Promise Ridge; or about the time the harvest cook put two cups of salt into the cake by accident. Acy was a good harvest hand and first to the table. He gobbled up the cake without a flinch. In a word, the man is slow. For this, he is in everyone's care. He is the local character helping the citizens of Wallowa measure their responsibilities.

They say that once at a City Council meeting, Acy Deucy came up on the agenda. As I heard the story several times in Wallowa (where word travels fast and often), Acy's custom was to walk into town Saturday, celebrate until he could barely stand, then sleep it off in the fire station and walk home to Promise on Sunday. For the City Council, this routine became grave.

"When he pulls out those hoses to make a nest for himself," said one, "he jeopardizes the response time of the crew. If they get a call on a Saturday night, they'll have to untangle him before they can jump on the truck and go."

"I've been thinking on that," said another. "When you're talking fire, you're talking life and death. Let's lock the station so he can't get in. I've tried, but you can't reason with that man on a Saturday night."

"If we leave the door open to Acy," a third replied, "we *might* lose a house or even a life to a fire; if we lock the door, we will *surely* lose Acy to the cold. The man will freeze."

They all thought for a time, and then voted to leave the door open as it had been. And there Acy sleeps every Saturday night.

The obvious solution of leaving a mattress or blanket in the fire station for Acy's use never occurred in the several versions of this story I heard. Nor did I ever meet anyone who had actually attended the Council meeting where this discussion was supposed to have taken place. Whether the meeting occurred or not, however, the often-repeated account of the meeting serves as a parable for Wallowa residents. In this story the town sees itself playing a gamble of one life—no matter how peripheral and strange—against all the codes and procedures for public safety and efficiency.

One Saturday night I sat by Acy, his big hat hunched over the bar at Baird's Tavern. While the shuffleboard puck slid the length of its table on cornmeal, and two women leaned back to laugh about something one had whispered, while jacked-up cars rumbled slow as autumn down the street outside, Acy began to tell me about his dog, way out at the shack on Promise Ridge, waiting for his return.

"But these schools!" he said suddenly. "They'll be our death!" The bar got quiet for a moment. He swirled the beer in his glass to center the foam, then drained it. "My dog," he said softly, "my dog's a good dog. He just waits inside that cabin no matter how long I'm gone."

I FIRST MET Abe Johnson, the bird man of Cline Falls, in the Bend bus station. He had a fifty-pound sack of birdseed slung over his shoulder, a blue stocking cap on his head, and a smashed and greasy cowboy hat on top of that. The pockets on his long canvas coat were torn, and when he took a little jump to shift the load, corn and sunflower seeds scattered from his pockets onto the floor. He set his quart styrofoam cup of coffee onto the end of a crowded bench and began to talk. When everyone else turned away, he turned to me.

"It's the inner-outer!" He raised his dirt-gloved hands in supplication toward me. "It's empathy! That's what makes the birds come in." The woman hiding behind her novel glanced up. The kid in a black T-shirt with sleeves torn away looked over his shoulder from pinball. "Some days they don't want to. They hop around in those trees like they'll never come. But then. . . ." When Abe paused dramatically to straighten up, the sack fell off his shoulder and tipped the cup from its perch. As coffee ran like a gullywasher down the bench, two children, a ski bum, and an old lady leaped from the coffee's path down the trough of polished oak, but Abe never noticed: ". . . then they come right here to my shoulder," he said. "Right here!" He patted his left shoulder, and his face bloomed with joy toward an invisible chickadee. Between his pursed lips was a magic kernel of corn.

Someone appeared from the snack bar with a handful of paper napkins, and began with loud sighs to mop coffee from the bench. The old lady picked up Abe's empty cup, turned toward him with a chickadee's deference, then set the cup on top of the newsstand beside him and retreated. The boy's pinball game started to ring and jangle, and Abe brought his eyes into focus on me again.

"One time it was about ten degrees and snowing, but I

wanted this magpie to come land on my back." Abe bent down, and let his arms dangle like weeping willow vines. "Magpies are funny. They get it in their mind they won't come, and stubborn!" Abe suddenly flung his arms outward and let out a screeching magpie oath.

"Skeee! Skeeee!" The old woman, twenty feet away across the lobby, backed two paces to the wall. Abe brought his hands up against his heart, and twisted his neck to face me. "That's where the empathy comes. I started to feel it. Sweat dropped off my nose to the snow, I wanted it so bad. And ten degrees!" His fingers snapped into a prayer-clench, and his eyes closed. His lips trembled, then suddenly his eyes smiled open.

"There he came! That magpie didn't want to, but he did. Landed right on my spine and stayed. Hopped around and squalled like he'd hit the Promised Land." Abe sat down on the sack of birdseed, but immediately they called the Portland bus and he struggled to his feet, swung the sack to his shoulder with a fast wheeze of breath, and ambled toward the gate.

As the bus headed north on Highway 97, headlights punching the dark, most passengers settled in for sleep. Or they pretended to. Abe snorted and leaned across the aisle toward me.

"One time I was down on my belly for hours watching this beetle—little blue fella with knobby antlers. I followed him all afternoon, and must have covered fifty feet in circles and zags. That little guy had to work! Watching him, you get to know what it's like to flop onto your back and wrestle around trying to get up. I wanted to help him, but I couldn't. Held a twig out once for him to grab, but then I pulled it away. I wasn't his guardian, I was him! I forgot everything. Got soaked. Got stiff. Like I dozed, like hypnotized, like born bug! And all of a sudden, this crow lights on my shoulder, jumps down to snatch that beetle, and goes! I heard his beak crunch down, felt I was the one to die. Had a hard time getting up, too."

Abe got off in Redmond, and I saw him flop his load into the basket of a tricycle with a license plate, and pedal west in the dark. He started slow, but had achieved a steady, rambling rhythm by the time he left the pool of the station's tungsten light.

It was later I read about this man in the news, talked with his neighbors, began to learn the complex relation he has with the human community as a result of his attention to the wild birds. I learned of his confrontation with the gravel company that wants to scoop rock from under the bird sanctuary he has been informally developing for twenty-five years. A lawyer has donated time to stall the gravel operation. A local car dealership gave the three-wheeled cycle I had seen him ride. So far, the dentist Abe approached has declined to fix his teeth so he can whistle the proper songs to bring in the birds, but community pressure will be on him to do so.

Abe's work is not ranching or logging or transport or tourists or smoke jumping or any of the other mainstays of the Redmond community at large. His work is feeding the wild birds, diverting water from storm run-off to the trees they nest in, dragging home from the dump old appliances with which to fashion sculptural feed stations that invite the chickadees but keep the sparrows clear. For this, no matter how odd, he is a local saint.

One of his neighbors put it this way. When Abe stands like St. Francis—hands outstretched, a small bird on each palm, and the light of beatitude on his face, saying, "Here bird, here seed, come you little chatterbox"—anyone could see why others run interference for his needs in the world.

Several years after our meeting in Bend, I stepped through the juniper grove that surrounds his shack, calling out to warn him, "Mr. Johnson, are you there? Mr. Johnson, I met you once in Bend. Do you remember?" I stood before the shack, and heard something fumble around inside. The door scraped open a few inches and Abe's face appeared sideways. Then his hand reached out toward me holding a kettle of urine. He scowled.

"I don't like the look of that. Way too dark. What do you think?"

"It does look pretty dark," I said. "Hey, you were going to show me the birds."

"Birds?" His face, still sideways, softened to a toothless grin. "Give me a minute to get my boots on."

We carried on a shouted conversation through the door for close to a half hour while he sought the boots inside his box house, then he gave a mighty heave against the debris blocking the door, and got it pulled back far enough to slip through. He wore different hats this time, a short-billed hunter's cap and a tremendous broad-brimmed pilgrim affair on top. His pea-green coat sported six pockets bulging with seed that dribbled out when he twisted or bobbed to peer about. The zipper on his pants had failed, but two belts secured them, and the cuffs were stuffed into a pair of green rubber boots half a dozen sizes too large. Abe's sour fragrance trailed behind him like a river's fog, as he drifted through the tall grass before me from one feed station to the next.

"I came down from The Dalles in '48 to do potato harvest," he told me over his shoulder, "and stayed." He paused to smear a dab of peanut butter on the bark of a juniper tree well-darkened by his custom. "Been on this ground since." He led off again, this time toward a lone apple tree improbably alive among the dry-ground sage. Our path was not a line but a braid. We took the turnings of animals not intent to get somewhere but inquisitive to be everywhere. "There come sunflower." Abe pointed to a clump of dark green in the blond dead grass of July. "That's winterfood for chickadee. I haul it water from the river." We dropped into a ditch that led toward the apple tree. "I dug this ditch to pull the storm-water down off the rim. May lose that tree, though." The trunk stood on a little ring of flat ground Abe had sculpted for it. It had never been pruned or sprayed, living as Abe did by sheer intensity. There were no apples, and the tree didn't cast much shade. He put his hand on the trunk. "Woodpeckers starting to favor it. Bad sign."

The next feed station was an upright, cylindrical water heater laced with rust, with a stack of automobile brake drums on top. He lifted them down one by one, scattered fresh seed from his sack on a pan, then replaced the brake drums.

"These rims keep the sparrows off," he said, tapping the top brake drum with his fingernail. "They can't hang upside down and hop inside like a chickadee can. None of your upright birds can get in here. Just chickadees, and snag bird—little wren."

There was a small wind beside my ear, and a chickadee

lighted on Abe's left shoulder. Instantly, a sunflower seed appeared between his lips. The chickadee snatched it and was gone. The whole move between them had the quick grace of something choreographed many chickadee generations back.

We paused at a dead refrigerator in a juniper tree's deep shade. The door handle was gone, but Abe thrust his thumb through the rusted hole where the handle had been, and the door popped open. He reached inside to replenish the seed in his pockets, then shut the door with his knee. We climbed the slope, which was jumbled with shards of basalt the size of cars haphazard in a wrecking yard, to the garden. Here Abe had hauled horse manure in sacks on his back to form a level ribbon of soil winding along the slope of lichen-brightened rock. He had planted sunflower, tomato, potato, and corn, and from a cleft behind an old juniper he took a hoe and began to weed.

I sat in the shade and watched. My camera seemed the toy of another century. My hands were too clean to coax leaves from rock, as Abe did. In his hands, a rusted coffee can mended with pitch was Paleolithic. The day went dumb with calm. As he reached up to handle a flower head, his face was Inca. His coat was tree bark a wren searched for stray seed. Here at the place Abe lived, I was like other ungainly citizens of the modern bus ride. In this garden, we were the strange ones. On this earth, on his home ground, I was apprentice to Abe.

OVER ON THE WET SIDE, mossy deep in the coast range west from Eugene, Tubby Beers lived on Indian Creek with his team of Percherons, and his World War II tank for gypo logging parked in the front yard. The tank's turret had been removed, and in its place a home-welded boom of steel was hinged for swivel-work yarding logs. Tubby said with that rig he didn't need roads.

"Long as I'm in second-growth, I go anywhere I want. Course, if I want to be gentle about it, I use the horses. They don't leave more skid trail than a short-tailed rainstorm."

Tubby himself had to step sideways through some doors, and it's hard to believe he ever died. He seemed too vibrant to slip through the frame of a grave and be gone.

Inside the house that day, when a big laugh closed his eyes and I could frankly glance around, my gaze swept the world map taped to the ceiling; the fiddle, mandolin, and guitar hung handy on the wall; the eight stuffed animals crouching hospitably at eye-level on the living room shelf: bear, skunk, weasel, and related kin. The tribe of the wild lived inside Tubby's mind.

"There were seven men there that day," he began in a rush, "and they're all dead and my daddy told me and I'm the only one that knows." In the wake of those words could be the story of Tubby's Uncle Mike riding with Jesse James. Or Uncle Frank serving as Teddy Roosevelt's personal bodyguard in the battle of San Juan Hill. Or the Beers family fife and drum corps parting the sea of buffalo as they crossed the plains by wagon. Or a tale of Tubby's own shenanigans at rodeos and logging shows, and other lively celebrations, of Saturday nights riding his horse and roaring wild up-canyon from the Indianola Bar, blasting the sky with his guns for joy.

This time it was none of those. It was the tale of Madera's Grave, the story of a strange and crazy man who was saint in this place before Tubby was born. Lyman Madera built his cabin without a door, as Tubby told it, and had to climb in through a hole in the roof each night to sleep. He lost his son, he prayed, he died with a mountain named for him. That was all. After the story, Tubby plucked his guitar from the wall and prepared to sing.

"Don't write this down," he said, tuning up. "I just want you listening." The song was a terrible fervent thing about the Japs and honor and the flag and our young people today. His tear-filled eyes held mine.

Tubby lived alone, and all his love of things old or musical or wild showed around the house and yard: the five pair of cowboy boots muddy around the stove to dry—all his; the saddle flung over the porch rail; the Percherons sidling eagerly into harnessing position when he stepped toward them. His great hands grabbed the tail of each and pulled. They tensed, but stood unmoved.

Besides his long stories and songs and asides, up a little side canyon Tubby kept a secret for us all. He got quiet and led me out the door and away through the trees to a hidden barn. Inside, he had kept oiled and polished ready for work an entire set of horse-drawn farm machinery. It was a museum in a barn that no one knew but the few he led there. He was historian for the primitive life. He was scholar with no degree or say-so but what he knew was crucial.

"They're all dead and I'm the only one that knows."

FARTHER WEST, just over the dunes from the Pacific, Marge Severy kept her home alone. The first time I stopped by, she had mushrooms spread fragrant on the kitchen table to dry—

the Japanese pine mushroom that grows only on the slopes of Mount Fuji and on this coast, she said to me.

As one of the last of the local Siuslaw Indian people, she was the original character of the valley. We were the odd ones, the eccentric citizens of this landscape—with our motorized processions and neon fantasies strung out along Highway 101. When a low fog hung over the river and fir trees bowed down with rain, when old swans called from the south dunes and cormorants came winging low over town, I saw her walking. She was a part of those proper customs by fog and bird song. She was with the place, and we were strangers to it. We might one day belong as she had always.

She sat on an overturned boat one Sunday afternoon, watching the university archeologist dig out bones and beads and slender shells, fragile as ash, from a grave at the heart of town. Someone, digging a sewer line, had found the grave. Now it was being removed and labeled for study. The man worked in the shade of his pit, and Marge, the sun behind her, wore the halo light of the old and the quiet. There was coherence in the earth. The man with the trowel and screen laid a ruler in the grave, and numbered everything he took away.

We met again at the Indian cemetery Marge cared for, across from her house up North Fork. I found her leaning on a hoe among the wooden markers and indistinct plots in the sand. Fog rolled down over a tremendous dune above us.

"Soon that will be here," she said, gesturing toward the dune. "Pretty soon I won't be watching over these old graves. That will be kind of a relief, you know, because then nobody can dig them up to study them, like they do to our people."

SOMETIMES before first light, when I stand behind my house in the city to listen, those hermit names come easy to my mouth. I will be one of them. For I would live their code of poverty and imagination in a doorless patchwork house guarded by a ferocious goose. I would live by the miracles of the uninsured. I would walk only, I would speak for days only with the birds, I would sing, and tend my village with a hoe.

Maybe it's jail by now for Gypsy Slim. Maybe it's death. Maybe it's a campsite, somewhere in my life.

RIVER
& ROAD

AN EARLY OREGON LAW named each navigable river an official
state highway. Among these was the Siuslaw, running west from
the coast range into the sea. Where the river curved and shouldered against bluffs, a road was impossible in the early days, and
traffic went by water—up from Florence at the coast, to Mapleton near the head of tide-water, fifteen miles inland. There was
a kind of road threading along the ridge above the north bank,
but locals called it The Goat Trail, and it was a shocker compared to the easy glide of flat water. The river was there; a real
road might someday be made. Houses faced the water.

The river made a lot of sense, and a pioneer could make
sense too, by figuring out the river. Salmon came up the river,

logs came down. The best farmland was right against the water.
Every morning, the milk boat came by, then the fish boat, then
the school boat, then the mail boat, and now and again, the
schooner from San Francisco. Before wildcat logging clogged
the channel with silt, two-masted schooners could float all fifteen miles inland to Mapleton. If you weren't on the river with
a dock in good repair, you just weren't part of modern life.

Rain, a glory of rain made the river the natural ribbon that
bound everything up like a purse-seine slung across the hills.
The river was everywhere—not a place, but a way of happening. Charlie Camp told me how the two happy tourist ladies
from California stopped to talk. They got on the subject of rain.

"How much rain do you get here, Mr. Camp?"

"Oh," he said, "we get about eight foot a year. That's
common, but I've seen more."

"Now, sir," said one of the ladies, "just because we come
from California, we don't need to believe that." They liked their
old Oregon man.

"Ladies," he said, "you see that elderberry bush down
there by the barn? That's eight foot tall. If we took our year's
fall of rain in a day, that bush would be under the flood."

Was he right? He was. Mapleton, Oregon, right up against
the west jump of the coast range, combs off ninety-six inches of
rain in a common year. That's nothing compared to the twenty
feet of rain that falls on the west slick of the Olympic Peninsula
to the north, but it's wet. Charlie told me you know you're in
Oregon when you can stand on the porch and grab a salmon
fighting its way up through the thick tumble of the rain. That
turned into a song as I drove home:

Step to the porch, a salmon flies by—
Hook him in out of the rain.
You're pretty far gone, pretty far gone:
You're clear out here in Oregon.

When a baby is born, as everyone knows,
There's moss in its fingers, webs in its toes.
It's pretty far gone, pretty far gone—
It's clear out in Oregon.

There is the chill glory of baptism by rain every day of winter when you step outside. So why not use that water for a road?

One well-schooled pioneer played a little dance with the river out of sheer practicality. He staked his homestead claim on the good farmland up North Fork, but when he came to look for timber up to his high standard, he found nothing close by. Seeking the tree, he cruised four miles down North Fork to the Siuslaw channel, then a good twelve miles upriver to Mapleton, then another mile south up Knowles Creek. There he stood, a good fifteen miles from home as the crow flies, but the tree he found was too straight and the water too handy to do it any other way. He felled the tree parallel to the creek, and bucked out one good forty-foot log, five-foot through at the little end. He rolled that log to the bank of Knowles Creek with the help of a logging jack, a tool that stood about knee-high and asked for patience. Then he carved his brand on the butt end of the log, left instructions at the sawmill downstream, and went home to his tent.

When high water came in the spring, Knowles Creek rose, picked up his log sweet as you please, and carried it a mile down to the main channel of the Siuslaw at Mapleton. From there, the log made its own way downstream to the mill above Point Terrace, where it was identified, barked, slabbed off, and run through the saws. The mill filled the order matched to the brand, took its own percentage of lumber out for the trouble, and stacked what was left on the riverbank.

When the moon was right and the tide deep, the man drifted down North Fork of a morning, rode the flood tide up the Siuslaw to the mill by skiff, dressed his lumber into a raft at slack tide, then herded it downriver on the ebb. The next turn of the tide put him off the mouth of North Fork, and he spent slackwater turning his raft into the North Fork channel. When the next flood tide swung in, he rode his raft by dark up North Fork until he came to his claim. A nice two-story house came out of that one log, with siding left over for the barn, and the man passed on easy ways to his children.

He took the time, he knew the ways. The river did the rest.

The early drift-netters on the Siuslaw suffered under two delusions that sweetened their lives considerably. I talked with Trygve Nordhal, who remembered both. First, it seemed obvious that any motor on the boat would scare off the fish. Second, salmon can see, right? By day, they would surely stay out of any net you laid down. So the word went. So drift boats went by spruce oars only, and by night. You had to know every tree on the dim night-sky horizon, sight them against the starlit clouds to turn and turn, to stay in the channel clear.

Every stretch of good driftwater on the river had a name. There was the Barney Drift, where old Indian Barney once fished. There was the Squaw Drift, and to the side of it, little Papoose Drift, then the Town Drift, Woodpile, Stickpatch,

Sandpile, Spruce Point, The Homestead, and Deep Hole Drift where the salmon crowded the deep channel against the north bank. At the Barney Drift, the best of them all as Tryg told it, "We'd go out about twenty oarstrokes, and then we'd lay net, and drift down to what we called The Gap, and pick up the net. Then we'd lay out again, and drift down to what we called The Three Shorts. And that was the end of the ebb-tide drift."

Talking of fish and the river, Trygve's voice spoke with the rush and ebb of water. There was the turbulent haste of his knowing words, then a milling around at slack, then a drift back down for ebb: "Early in the season, we'd go whenever the tides were right. If it was a minus tide in the evening, we'd fish below the bridge—if it was high tide in the evening, just about dark, why the fish would make it across the bar, clear up to North Fork before you caught them, and you couldn't catch a fish below the bridge. They never stopped. They came on the tide as far as they could. If it was low water in the evening, for some reason they came in on the morning tide, they flew around, and went back down for a minus tide—low water in the evening, first dark. But if it was high water in the evening, you could not catch a fish below Florence on high water slack. They'd all be up to Barney Drift. They'd catch a hundred fish to the boat up here. You wouldn't catch one below the bridge. They move in cycles like that. And you catch more fish if it wasn't raining. If it was raining, they'd move right up the river. Seemed like they don't go up the river until they have some fresh water."

The nets were twenty-five meshes deep for the lower river, thirty meshes deep for the upper channel. Meshes ran eight inches for Chinook salmon, six and three-quarters for silverside, six and a quarter for fall steelhead. Fishermen who didn't know the river spent their days mending net they'd trailed into snags. Not only the drift sites had names, but the hidden snags as well. Trygve: "Right off the Town Drift, downstream side, you had to pick up fast. A big spruce tree had fallen in the river there years ago, and it had The Eagle's Nest, they called it. Would just about take your whole net, if you got caught in that."

In one night with a set net, a farmer on the river could catch enough of the big Chinook to last all winter. One Chinook would fill several gallon jars for salt-fish, and a net could pick forty fish from the river in one night. No one recorded the Siuslaw Indian names for these fishing sites, but with a river so rich, they may have been similar to what Franz Boas recorded for the Kwakiutl candlefish stations way north: "Full in Mouth," "Fat," "Eating Straight Down," "Eating All," "Eagle Bowl," "Owning Many," "Place of Succumbing." When a Kwakiutl mother bore twins, she knew they were salmon; if they came near water, they might take off their human masks and swim away.

On the Siuslaw, when fall rain failed to fill the river deep, the grocery schooner from San Francisco couldn't make it in across the bar. Then people ate salmon and potatoes three times a day, every day, all winter long. Like the Siuslaw people before them, those pioneers ate the river.

Salmon came up, logs came down. There is one house on Cox Island with no road but the river—the Sanborne house, now windowless and sagging. Mrs. Sanborne told me how she stood by the top window at dusk, and saw her husband float past in a raw December storm, hopping from log to log on a big billowing raft that had broken loose. He glanced once at her lamp-lit shape, waved, and then turned furious to his work and drifted darker downstream west. That time, he lived.

Fred Buss told me how the river took a life. The tug was coming in to dock, and the crowd on shore was as turbulent as the water. People simply jostled Miss Sherman loose from balance, and down she went from the pier. A young man shucked his hat and went in after her, swam under the keel, but came up alone.

Miss Sherman had just become engaged, Fred said, and that softened his way with the story some, but he told it stroke by stroke as an oarsman would who lived by killing the river's fish and knowing its way.

"We watched for her three nights, thinking she'd come to our nets as others had, and every time we pulled in heavy, reached for some silver arm of fish by the lamp-box, it might be her. Fish drown, too, in the net, you know. They come in stiff, cold. And sometimes salmon come to the lamp, up out of the channel, and drop away again. But Miss Sherman stayed down three days.

"Then we were mending net on the dock in the morning. My partner says, 'We'll see Miss Sherman soon. She ought to be floating by now.' And by God, there she comes, slow past our dock on the ebb, face down, white bump on the water. I was for putting a net out, but these damn fools had to turn her over with an oar. Of course her face was gone. Crabs had eaten that, breasts and all. I said to let her be, but they would not. Jesus, it made me mad. As she rolled up, her left fist came out of the water. There's her gold ring then, hanging by the fingerbone."

WHEN THEY finally paved a road down the north bank of the Siuslaw, Ted Bugbee was foreman. One December morning when the river was ice, he got plain disgusted with the hand-tools he'd been given to use—sledges, picks, and shovels rusted dull, split hickory handles taped but raw with splinters.

"Boys," he said, "let's pitch our tools into the river, and see if I can't get us a new set from the boss. Ready? All together now—heave ho!" With the shouts and laughter of a good drunk, the boys flung out, and tools went skittering onto the ice but stayed. The ice that day ran too thin to walk on, but too thick to let the tools drop through. Ted had a problem. Should the boss come by, it could be tough to explain how those tools came to lie on the long silver road of the Siuslaw.

"With rocks—sink 'em!" Rocks it was, the ice shattered, and the old tools were gone.

"Break time, boys. Start a fire. I'll be back." Ted went straight to the boss, just waking in his Mapleton hotel.

"Say, Boss, the boys are in a hell of a fix down there. No tools to speak of, and they're standing idle. Hate to see that. Shall I swing by the hardware for a new set? Fine. Right, Sir. Sorry to wake you, Sir."

IN THE CITY, a hundred miles from the Siuslaw, I wake to the whisper and throb of the freeway—Interstate 5, a lit ribbon one-quarter mile north. Once when I complained of its noise, as I opened the window on a June evening and the freeway roared, my wife's mother said, "Pretend you are hearing the river."

The river, yes. Her words were wise. I thought I could school my ears to that memory of water's grace. I would hear the whisper of the road, and I would learn to remember one pioneer, drifting down the Siuslaw in a skiff of split cedar—the man who shot a swimming bear, then dove to the riverbed to pull its sleeping form up by the ear. But my heart was weak. In the night, I burrowed into the seashell of my pillow, but the whisper I heard was not water. I dove for the secret turmoil of dreams. The road's urgent drone, the whine of speed, the growl of trucks gearing down to climb—all that swarm of noise would not soften to a watersound for me. Try midnight, try three before dawn: the same.

The road is a frozen river that never thaws.

When I stand on the overpass bridge and look down, I can see how water designed the freeway road. Six lanes follow a canyon water carved, a canyon aimed east, then north toward the Willamette River. On-ramps join the road and thicken it, like generous tributaries in spate. There is a tidal ebb in the commuter rush at dawn downstream toward the city, then noon slack, and then flood-tide dusk, when the lit eyes of the silversides fight their way back up-canyon, sniffing for the exact small pool where they shall spawn. Where north- and south-bound lanes divide, an island hides in the road with pines and a deep thicket of blackberry. From above, I can see where drifters have built their campfire and slept on cardboard.

I've found the equivalent of beach-drift on that road bank: lengths of stovewood bounced from a truck, exotic weeds sprung from gravel, skidded ears of corn, greasy wrappers glittering like fish bones. One day I slowed for a great blue heron poised by the median ditch. Birds haunt the road, hawks on posts, starlings billowing. Do high geese follow the freeway north, now that it runs as geographic ribbon brighter than the river? My cousin saw the long column of migrating butterflies flickering above that road, bound south for Mexico. All day, they clogged the grilles of cars.

Driving the freeway south one winter day, I pulled over where a woman stood with her thumb in the wind. She was an old hand at this, I saw at once, as she stepped in front of my Malibu to hold me still while she checked me out through the windshield. Then she opened the door.

"How far?" she said, wanting the tone of my voice to tell if I was dangerous.

"I'm going to Salem—forty miles."

"Okay for a start." She climbed in, sandals on her feet, feathers in her hair. We set out. I waited for the story that is a hitchhiker's ticket. Ten miles passed in silence. As we cruised out over the freeway bridge, crossing the Willamette, she spoke.

"Wow. This river has probably been here a long time."

"Yeah," I said. "A while."

"Do you think," she said, "it's been here two hundred years?" I studied her face for a smile. None. At Salem, she stepped out without a word.

ONE FOG-NIGHT I slept on an island in the river: watersound and cold. I snuggled deep in my bag and dreamed. In my dream was a wizard wearing a five-pronged bronze ring. He called it "the perfect ring of beauty and evil." Whoever wore the ring could see into another as God sees, could see that soul as a perfect ring—shining, flawed, forgiven. There was dance, set to the pentameter chant of a hunting song that named the animals.

It stopped. I struggled for the ring—it was on my finger. I turned to my partner: eyes and hair of a naked soul, luminous hands raised up, her heart wild with pleasure and grief.

Watersound woke me. Dark. I was ready to lie there season by season, to die from my life, or to live as the river lives, to climb with salmon and fall away from that final loving work like rain, to tumble headlong, to flicker away silver with light, powered by moon and sun.

DANCING BEAR
OF THE SIUSLAW

WHY SO MANY STORIES about bear? When I was little, my brother came home from summer-camp and told me. They ran a bear down with dogs, he said, shot it, dragged it to camp, skinned it out while a ring of children looked on. A skinned bear looks most like a man, my brother said. He lay there at the hub of their silent circle, the ragged disguise of his blood-matted fur bundled away. He was a man.

That's the heart of it. Bear is our silent partner in the wilderness. In this century of our ways, bear keeps an honesty. Since President Teddy, our children carry small, furry souls to bed. Far from home, I dreamed of the marriage of bear and woman, and I was comforted. The sun was hot, the grass was wet: "Will you be my love today?" she said. "Will you be my love today?" Waking from that was sweet. Something had been healed. If I lived alone, I believe I would gradually take on the mossy costume of bear, the rank scent and ungainly grace of that dancer standing to sip wind. They tell me that an Eskimo, exiled for education to the state of Washington, tramped into the mountains seeking something to teach him respect. Books had it not, nor wise teachers. The city was tinsel. He sought bear.

When I did oral history in the Siuslaw Valley on the central Oregon coast, bear kept weaseling into stories.

"You know," said bachelor Charlie Camp, "they used to wrestle bear, down here at the service station in Mapleton. I worked on the railroad, tamping ballast and driving spikes. It was real boring work, but I got used to it, I guess. Night in town was for bear. It was a switch from days. Right there at the north end of the covered bridge they kept him muzzled, with a kind of boxing mittens of rawhide covering his claws. He was chained, too, so he had enough handicap to even things out. These big loggers used to bet heavy they could pin him before the clock ran out. Thing was, he wouldn't stand. If he'd stand, they could usually knock him down. But he'd hunch tight and they rode him, then he'd roll and the boys would really squall."

Crickets chirped in Charlie's house, and a log truck thundered past. The clock worked a while in solitude. "A few guys beat him, but a lot got broken bones. That bear learned to get a turn of his chain around a guy's body, and then he won every time. So they decided to turn him loose inside the garage for a night match. That bear steamed in his pen, and when the first challenger stepped up, they pulled the trap door open. Trouble was, he'd lost all fear of man. Went on a rampage and right away the lights got knocked out and everybody went to growling and clubbing each other on the fur-top thinking it was bear. Somebody got the door open, and he was gone. They found a mitten down by the cannery but never saw the bear again. A little afterward, we got a movie theater, and had little socials and things. Somehow, nothing was quite fun like bear."

Charlie glanced out the window at his pet cow. A tire hung from a maple tree for the cow to scratch its back on. Inside, gray underwear festooned the furniture.

"I'm a bachelor," he said, "and I live like a bachelor."

Another old-timer down the road, Dan Miles, trapped his first bear when he was eight. The trap itself was so big, he couldn't carry it alone. Bear lard, he said, made the best pie crust in the world. He remembered skinning out bear in the fall with fat so thick you could bury your hand in it, and he still kept a jar of the finer grease to keep rust off his saws.

"I chased a swing donkey one winter," he said, "when we had a pole-road up in that Luckiamute country. Pole-road's a chute for running logs down off a hill into water. You fasten two big logs on the sides, and two little ones in the trough— run that chute half a mile down the slope sometimes. Lay your logs in at the top and they skid the trough clean to the river.

"There was a man—I guess it was the truth, because he brought a whole lot of his crew down and they all claimed it— said they shot a bear with one of them logs. It was when they had their lunch down at the foot of their pole-road. And that old bear knew to come around after lunch to clean up the scraps. That's when they always managed to leave enough scraps for the bear. Well, they get up top, and they turn in these whole bunch of toots on the whistle, so that bear could know to get out of the way. That bear started across the foot of the pole-road just as they turn in this whole bunch of toots. Thought he could make her across, but he never made her. That log went through just like a bullet.

"And sometimes the logs went so fast they had to drive marlin spikes in the trough to slow them down. Logs ran so fast, the shavings flew twenty feet high, chiseling out of the heads of them spikes."

Dan eased back and was done. I didn't have to believe. I knew the story was true, we got such a quiet joy from it. His wife came in from making applesauce.

"That's not right," she said. "Tell about your schooling." But he would not. His first wife had been killed by a logging truck. Her first husband died falling from a spar tree. They had married within the week of both events, being well in the habit of living with someone.

"Got so damn lonely," as Dan said. Friends complained, but they two knew how it was. Death helps tell you how to live.

Another logger killed a sow bear by the bad luck of falling a tree on her. Bucking out the log, he found her sprawled under it, and twin cubs burrowing in to suckle her still. This made him think of his own daughter. He carried the cubs home, wrapped warm in the skin of their mother. One died, one lived chained in the yard. That logger's daughter was the natural envy of her friends, until the bear began to grow. That's the old story then, some wild maturity the world can't handle. That morning came when her bear hugged her hard, would not let go, she screamed, her mother came with an iron frying pan and killed the bear with one blow.

Bear stories always seem to be about two things, about bear and a partner. It may be a dream partner of some meaning. For Charlie, bear was counterpart to the sheer boredom of railroad work. For Dan, bear was partner to the marvel of traveling logs. For the logger, cub was brother to his daughter. The brotherhood of bear and self came most clearly from the mouth of Martin Christensen, trapper at eighty-three on Tsiltcoos Lake.

"I used to hunt bear too," he said. "Killed my share. But once, you know how the old loggers left stumps fifteen, twenty foot high? They'd springboard up, and saw clean through. Left that kinky wood in the butt-swell stand, and just hauled the straight trunk to the mill. They came back later and harvested the stumps, once they figured how to use them. Anyway, I used to sit up on one of them stumps where I could see along a bear trail, and I'd wait. At berry time, bear walks almost drunk, rambling in a fog of his own pleasure. That's the time to kill them, I thought. Kill 'em happy, fat. Fellow has a family, kids. You get to thinking that way.

"Foggy morning early, I was sitting on my stump. My hunting buddy had gone on into the swamp to a stand of his own. Just a pinch of sun came through, and I sat still, with my gun cradled across my knees. I'd seen bear sign all along that run—pretty open ground for a hundred yards each way. You know, hunting's like prayer when you live it right. You get to expect something so strong, it comes to you. And I just expected that bear out through a young stand of hemlock. He came ambling down the trail to me, dew on his ears, salal on his mind. He'd have been humming if he was a man.

"Up on my stump, I was a good fifteen foot off the ground, and that baffled my scent. When the bear came close he found something in the wind and stood up. First he turned slow to look back down the trail. Then he swiveled around, his eyes squinted shut to give his nose more play, kissing the wind and blowing steam. I hadn't moved, but he found me, sitting high as a damn totem pole. He opened his eyes and we looked at each other. The sun burned through, and his face fur glistened. I knew I ought to raise my gun and shoot him. He knew he ought to drop and run. But we held. We held there. I was looking into something. I was looking into the face of a man. Maybe he saw bear in me, bear with a little stink of gunmetal. He finally eased down and went on. Fog closed in behind him. When I heard a shot from way off in the swamp, I felt a chill to my back as if that bullet grazed me.

"I been hunting a lot of years. I still trap some. But my days hunting bear, they're done."

WHEN THE INDIANS were mostly gone from the Siuslaw, bear became the truest local citizen. When bear dwindled, pioneers come too late had to invent Sasquatch to act that necessary part of the wild one. Charlie, Dan, Martin had no need for Sasquatch. Bear was the mask of their own souls got loose in the woods. The lore of Sasquatch is thin gruel to the hot old food of bear stories. One night someone brought a Sasquatch movie to the Siuslaw. We crowded the school gym, hoping to be terrified, but the film made us laugh. It was all a dark blur of underexposed night shots—faces glittering with sweat by the flicker-light of campfires as something screamed from the forest and actors tried to act afraid.

True bear stories are otherwise. A true story rises irrepressible from the place itself. I learned this from a book and from a mouth. I can't remember the face around the mouth, or the name of the teller. Only the story the book brought back to mind. First, the book, a linguist's text: *Siuslawan*, the fortieth volume in the *Handbook of American Indian Languages*.

In March of 1911, Leo Frachtenberg, a student of Franz Boas, came to the Oregon coast to study the language of the Siuslaw Indians. He didn't go to the Siuslaw Valley itself, where Charlie and Dan and Martin lived then young, because most of the original tribe had been moved north to the Siletz Reservation. As Frachtenberg reports, "besides the four individuals who served as my informants [at Siletz], and the two or three Siuslaw Indians said to be living near Florence, Lane County, there are no other members living; and since these people no longer converse in their native tongue, the Siuslaw family may be looked upon as an extinct linguistic stock." At Siletz, Frachtenberg laboriously wrote out two original texts from the speaking of Louisa Smith, an old woman nearly deaf. One is an invocation for rain. The other is the story of the dancing bear of the Siuslaw.

It begins, in Frachtenberg's literal translation, "Long ago. Very bad long ago world. Everywhere thus it started long ago. A bad person was devouring them. Grizzly Bear was devouring them long ago. When a man went out hunting, he would kill and devour him. People came together and desired to fix his disposition, to kill him always."

Since this bear could not be killed with arrows, the people decided to invite him to dance. While he danced, they might kill him. If he would dance until fatigue felled him, he might be killed. They sent a messenger to invite him, but he would not come without a gift. A gift is a promise. They promised a knife. The shrewd messenger said to him, "You are my relative. Why don't you want to go?"

"I am wise, that's why I don't want to go. It seems to me I am simply wanted there to be killed. That's why I am wise." But at last Bear said, "All right, I will go. I don't care, even if I die."

At the dancing, he was still suspicious. The people crowded around him with promises: "Friend, don't sleep. We will play. Don't sleep, O friend! Not for that purpose we asked you to come." But Bear grew sleepy, sitting by the great fire to watch the dancing.

"Don't sleep. Look on! For that purpose we invited you. We have abandoned all our hatred." They said, "Move away from the fire, you may get burned!"

But Grizzly Bear said, "Leave me alone. I intend to sleep a while."

Then a man stood over Grizzly Bear and took hold of the burning pitch. Bear lay sleeping.

"Better pour it into his mouth!" And as Grizzly Bear burned, the people danced. As he died, smoke rose.

"Here the story ends," said Louisa Smith. "If Grizzly Bear had not been killed, this would have been a very bad place.

Thus that man was killed. Such was the custom of people living long ago. Here at last it ends."

In the city library, I was a hundred miles and seventy years from Siletz. But under the hum of fluorescent light, tasting the words of Louisa in my mouth—*sqak wàn smîtu*, "here it ends"— I danced with the people and died with Bear. The smoke of that death bit thick. I reached out for those few Siuslaw people Frachtenberg never met, the remnants of that tribe the old settlers of Florence had told me about.

A white woman nearly slain with senility had said to me, "Oh, Indians, yes. I remember old Indian Dan, Indian Jeff. We named our dogs Dan and Jeff. They were wonderful dogs." The casual wander of the feeble mind had this terror to it: their story is done, as mine is nearly done.

But then in the library, I had to wonder if it really ends. *Sqak wàn smîtu?* Like Martin Christensen, I waited on a stump to know. Like the bear, I looked toward light with dim eyes. I remembered another story from the mouth whose name I could not remember. It was a story told about the people who drove Louisa Smith and her tribe from home ground. It was a story rising irrepressible from that ground. It went like this:

"Lots of homesteaders came who never stayed. Rain gets to you, mold in your socks. Fog so thick, babies cut their teeth on it. And one man, after years of trying to prove up his claim by Lily Lake, left the country without telling a soul. When the neighbors came by in the morning, his cabin was empty and that was all.

"Folks called his place the Red Bungalow—one big red-walled room, with a little sleeping room off the back. Right away it was the community's gathering place. That's where people came for parties. We could set up table and share a meal, then push everything out of the way and dance. Someone always had a fiddle: fire up the chimney, forget your troubles, and dance. Pretty soon, kids would be asleep in the back room, and then you may as well dance till dawn. No reason to risk your neck on the mud road by dark.

"One night when I was a kid, I woke up when something stopped the music. I came out into the big room rubbing my eyes. All the big folks stood there listening, looking at the ceiling or the fire, and some had moved to the open door or out onto the porch. I got out there too, before my mother could see me, and standing by the rail I could hear some pain squall way out across the water. There wasn't any storm, but it was blowing like it usually does, and a little rain, so you couldn't hear real clear, but something was pretty sorry out in the dark. First you'd hear wind buffet the roof, and then little waves slap the lake edge, and then that sound.

"I heard a man say it must be bear in a trap—that's about the direction where the Mercer boys ran their line. It must have been around midnight, and too dark to go chasing bear. 'Best let her be till light,' the man said. And pretty soon, the fiddle killed that sound, and everyone went in to dance some more.

"I got my blanket out on the porch and sat there listening. I'd doze a while, and then the wind or the fiddle would die away enough to wake me with that sound. It had some anger in it, but mostly plain sorry. In my head half asleep I could see the bear stop to listen to our fiddle, and stand up like we did to hear him cry. I saw him prance around, but I was sleeping. Once I heard people calling my name, but when my mother found where I was, she just bent down over me, left a taste in the air between whiskey and a rose, and went back to the dance. Long night then. The fiddler got drunk and the music changed. A man on an errand fell shouting in the lake, and seemed like some folks wore different clothes than they started with. The dancing faltered. It was still plenty dark, but everyone started packing to go home and milk the cows.

"Once the dancing really stopped, we heard the bear calling all the time, and it seemed to get on people's nerves. When one of the Mercer boys showed up with a gun, the other kids woke up. The Mercer boy's eyes were wild and happy, and the kids were all crazy to go with him. Someone picked up a fatwood torch. We started off slow, stumbling in the dark, then getting so close to the kid with the torch we nearly got singed. We went half around the lake, and came on the bear thrashing in a big dished hole he'd dug. We were pretty close and we could taste the bear smell that spooks horses. Then his eyes glittered. The trap chain hung shiny where he'd gnawed it, and the tree was stripped white. His right front paw was limp inside the jaws. Then he stood up.

"I had seen my father stand like that—when a stump would not come free from earth, or when a calf died for all the help he gave it. There was something in the bear's shoulders, though, besides fatigue. Something I wanted. Maybe every kid there felt the same, but I saw the bear looking at me alone.

"The bear turned to the one with the gun, and the Mercer boy put a bullet through its face. The bear dropped like a sack and lay still. For some reason, I was holding a stick, and the boy told me to go see if the bear was dead. I took the torch in my left hand, the stick in my right, and eased up toward the bear's wallow from the side. It was flattened in the shadow there. As I came up, it lay sprawled on its back like a furry open hand. I could see the wet glitter of one eye, one eye on me. Then it clouded, a sheen went out of it. I sat down on the edge of its grave. That's all."

YEARS AFTER I heard that story, my sister camped by Lily Lake. She didn't know about Grizzly Bear, or the Red Bungalow, then long sunk to earth. She had heard other stories. She had heard that a lonely woman guarded the place, and blew out the tires of trespassers with telepathy. She had heard only travelers with respect might stay past dark. My sister had heard enough to brighten her mind through a long night. Maybe this helped her hear the stamping, the chain of the dancer. It wasn't surf pounding to the west, she told me. Not her heart that woke her first. She looked into the moonlit face of her companion. Both knew it. Something irrepressible was trying to be remembered.

East, up Separation Creek in the Three Sisters Wilderness, my wife and I met a thin summer bear the second day of our honeymoon. We were in the sweet daze of that event, sidling along with packs too heavy and heads too light. How many bottles of wine does it take, how few words? We grazed on huckleberries as we went. And here came a bear doing the same. We passed each other on that fragrant trail in sun. We held a trust, a kinship in that month. Berries and honey, woman and bear—the world fit.

I think now of that mythic room in the voice of Louisa Smith, and the fog-walled room at Lily Lake. By such stories, we keep listening to the world itself. Next time we invite the bear to dance, neither partner needs to die.

My brother taught me the last story. Hiking the Three Sisters Wilderness alone, he saw the amorous bears rolling about in that meadow up by Lauder Mountain—the lupine crushed, Indian paintbrush flattened in their loving swathe, how he nibbled her ear and she smacked him with her paw, there in the fall of fat September. My brother crept away on hands and knees into the hemlock thicket, left them be. Sunlight struck the dancing bears, apart from our human way: this wearing of shoes, and words, and nations.

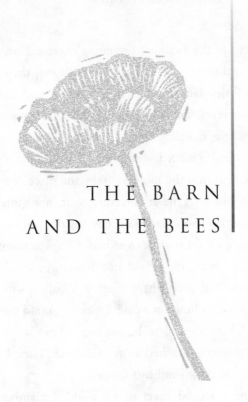

THE BARN
AND THE BEES

My parents and I were driving along Boone's Ferry Road early one Sunday morning with a ripe load of horse manure in the back of the family station wagon when we saw a hand-lettered sign nailed to a telephone pole: "2 x 4 is 25 cents, 2 x 6 is 50 cents." There was so much fog on the glass we had to open the side window to see an arrow in red crayon pointing up a road to the west. Even the steam from the hot stuff behind us couldn't blunt the chill that went through me. Up that road was a barn I had admired since I was a child, and I knew it had fallen. In the same moment I felt the thrill of honest greed.

Twenty minutes later I stood alone in the fumbled ruin of red boards, straw, and the sweet stink of old dairy. No one was around, except the swallows careening overhead where the eaves had been and their nests hung once. Like me, they clung to the vacancy of the familiar. Blackberry vines had held the barn upright for years, and now that it was down the vines trailed over the tangle, dangling in a veil from the south and east walls that still stood crooked somehow. I scrambled up a slanted timber wedged into the pile to survey the place. The deep litter I stood on had a fragile architecture to it, not quite fallen clear down in a crisscross balance of long sagging rafters propped in chaos, with bent tin roofing over half-collapsed rooms where the side bays had been, the rusted stanchions wrenched into twisted contraptions, and everywhere tangles of baling wire and splintered fir siding. The heap made a ticking sound as it settled in the heat. There seemed to be too much light on it all, the fragrant old mystery bleached away and done. Then I heard a low hum from the dark southeast corner.

Lifting a jagged sheet of tin aside, I clambered into the long tunnel of slanted posts and rafters down the nave, stepping from one nail-studded board to the next, putting my body through a snake's contortions without a snake's grace, every pop and squeak of wood on wood a warning, every ping of corrugated tin in the deadfall. I passed a boat filled with hay, its bow beached on a bale that sprouted green, its keel turned to earth. I passed a wagon with no wheels, split in half where a beam had dropped through its bed to the floor. Mice scattered before me, and a bumblebee struggled out from a ball of wool, its nest that had fallen gently to a new niche in the rusted skull-hollow of a drinking pan. I had to inhabit what was left of this palace before it came all the way down, and the bees were beckoning me from their half-shattered hive now thirty feet ahead.

Others were in church. I was in a trance. In the honey-sweet gloom of the back corner I stepped up onto a patch of floor. This dusty vestibule had the privacy of prayer, the solitude of visible history. The combs hung down from a four-by-four rough-cut brace on the wall, and the bees massed quietly there, working. The small back door opened onto acres of blackberry, and a thorned vine held it ajar with a double turn around the knob. Inside, a scatter of oats glittered on the threshold. A wheelbarrow stood mounded with jars. A currycomb worn down to nothing hung from a nail on the wall where each knot-hole was mended with the rusted lid from a tin can. If I stirred, my boot would crush broken glass, so I held still and watched the bees climb each others' backs to toil, to turn over pollen and flower-sap in their mouths in a flurry of wings and touch. The blunt, heavier shapes of a few drones waited among them to be fed—so inept they could not lick their own food from underfoot. The queen must have been on the inner combs, laying like mad at this season for the main summer honeyflow. From one mating flight, one meeting with a drone, she bore children all her life. If I stood in the dark, they would not bother me. It was light and work each gave her custom to, spinning out through the open door on the quickly tightening spiral of her errand.

I crawled out and away, the fragrance of the hive, the quiet of that dark corner filling me. Across a field, in what must originally have been the farmhouse, a neighbor of the barn in a heap gave me its owner's phone number, along with a sad look. "They finally got it," she said through the screen door, as she

brushed a wisp of hair aside. "I was hoping they'd forget to."
She was going to say more, but a child shouted and she closed
the door instead. Back home, I called and asked for Peter. I
knew it was best not to talk about money at first.

"Howdy," I said. "I was wondering about your plans for
the scrap from that barn off Boone's Ferry Road."

"Yeah?" he said. "Well I don't want anyone in there, the
shape it's in. On account of my liability."

"I can understand that," I said, "but I noticed some boards
piled out in front, and there *was* a sign about it."

"Sign? I didn't put up any sign. Must have been the guy I
hired to tear it down. We're stalled on account of some bees in
there."

"I can take care of those bees for you."

"Listen, you take care of those bees, and you can take anything you like. I've got to get everything out of there. Some guy
complained to the County about it being a fire hazard, and they
gave me a week. But do you really think there's anything worth
saving? What do you want it for?"

"I want to build a barn."

IN THE SHORT LIGHT at five a.m. I was there in my bee-gloves
and veil, mechanic's coveralls and tall rubber boots, threading
my way down the tunnel of boards and tin by memory and luck.
I carried a hive-box and a spray bottle of water and a soft brush.
Bees never sleep, but they generally don't fly when they're
chilled before dawn. I found them as they would be at that
hour, packed together on the combs with a low, sociable hum.
Once the sun hit that wall behind them, they would fly to work.

I stepped on the wrong board, the architectural balance above me groaned and shifted, a dozen bees lifted off with an altered pitch to their buzz, and the whole hive quickened. In their sudden, ordered turmoil, I was seeing a mood-change inside a friend's brain, something naked and fair. I waited without a word. Bits of straw flickered away as the guard-bees settled back onto the wall and climbed into the mass that quieted with their return. The warm scent of wax and honey came my way. Through the doorway, mist settled over the gray sweep of the blackberry meadow. It was in full blossom, and the bees must have been working it hard. I could see the white wax over capped honey cells whenever the mass of bees parted like a retreating wave from the comb's upper rim. There would be sweet enough to keep them alive once I dampened their wings, carved away the comb entire, and swept the chilled bees into the hive-box I carried. Through my veil I saw them in the cleft they had chosen, their little city compact with purpose in a neglected place.

By dawn I had them boxed, sealed tight and humming in the shade beside my car. A few had escaped my work, had followed me, then doubled back with the buzz of anger sinking to a different note. No one is quite sure what stray bees do when the home hive is destroyed and the swarm disappears without them. They might follow other bees to a foreign hive and try to take on its scent and be admitted. Or they might hang around the old vacancy, working the local blossoms and resting under a leaf until their wings are too frayed to hold in the air. Bees die when they sting, or when steady work finally shatters their wings.

Several days after the wall that had harbored the hive came

down, I would still see a few bees hovering precisely where the combs had been. At mid-afternoon I would turn over a board with the print of wax across its grain—some panel or brace that had boxed in the hive—and find a solitary bee fingering the pattern like a disbelieving relative reading by Braille the name new-carved on a tombstone. I shared their nostalgia for a shape in the air. And so did others, in their own ways. As I worked on that tangled lumber pile, neighbors came by in little groups or alone to leave with me some story about the barn, and to seek some scrap of it to carry away.

First came three boys to watch me work, to pick their way around the heap so glorious with its ramps and tunnels, its pedestals of triumph and hollows of secrecy. When the pile shifted under them, they leaped off and skittered away, then came back with their father from across the road. They wanted a treehouse made, and he wanted to see the barn. He was in his yard-work clothes, not in a hurry.

"You know, the woman that used to live in that old farm-house and own this barn was a strange one," he said to me, while the boys scattered again toward the ruin. "She'd show up at our place every fall to trade walnuts for whatever we had to trade. We always took the unshelled ones, her hands were so dirty. Or maybe they were dark from the hulling. She had gunny sacks tied around her feet with baling wire."

"When was this?" I asked.

"Before they were born." He gestured toward the three boys now waltzing along a beam thrust like a bowsprit from the pile. "Looks like I'd best get them home."

The four of them went away carrying the small roof from

the ventilator cupola. It had somehow stayed intact, riding the whole structure down as it fell, and ending perched on top of the heap. As they drifted across the road, they looked like four posts under the Parthenon.

Next came a gentleman in pressed yellow slacks and a shirt with a little alligator over his heart. His hands were clean and thin. He watched me labor for a while in silence.

"Hard work for a Sunday," he said. I stood up and let the sweat cool on my face.

"Well, I wanted to save some of these boards," I said. "The barn's gone, but there's some lumber left."

"Eyesore. I'm glad to see it finally come down." I looked at the mouth that had said this. I had nothing to say. Away across the pasture a solitary maple stood dark in its neglected shade.

"But say," he said, "I need a board to repair the rail on my deck—two-by-four, about twelve feet long. . . ." He skirted carefully around the perimeter of the pile, picking at the ends of likely boards clinched firmly into the weave of collapse, now and then looking my way appealingly. I knew who had called the County about the fire hazard, about the old barn settling too slowly deeper into moss and blackberry, the stack rattling in winter storms and the tin roof pinging through each summer's heat. I pulled an eighteen-foot clear-grained length of fir from the stack I had plucked of nails, and he went off with it at an awkward march, holding the board far out to the side of his body with his fingertips. Soon I paused in my work to hear the whine and ring of his powersaw toiling through the wood. I counted seven cuts, then silence.

The woman who had bought the farmhouse, who had given me the owner's name, came down to offer a glass of lemonade. The cold sweat from the glass ran down my wrist.

"I never let my kids go inside." She squinted into the patches of darkness where walls still leaned together. "They get into enough trouble as it is. But I always felt we owned the barn, along with the house—even though we didn't. You should have seen the place when we moved in: a car in the back yard filled with apples; a drawer in the kitchen packed with red rubber bands, and another with brown ones; mice in the walls and a possum in the attic. The house had been empty a long time too."

I set the glass down, and bent to my work, wrestling heroically with a long two-by-six mired deep in the hay.

"Are you going to keep these Mason jars?" She nodded toward a dozen blued quarts lolling in the grass.

"You'll use them before I do." I shook the sweat out of my eyes to watch her cradle eleven of them somehow in her arms, with one clenched tight under her chin. She started out with a crooked smile to walk hunched and slow up the lane toward a yard littered with bright toys.

"I'll come back for the glass," she called over her shoulder. Then she turned slowly, like a ship halfway out of harbor. "Or bring it up to the house for a refill."

The afternoon was a long season of history, a plunge into the archeological midden of my own Midwestern ancestors, a seduction of my hands by wood the flanks of the milkers polished. What was a stall of straw but a nest for stories, even under the naked, open light of the sky? Burlap lace around a jar blue with time held something without a name but kin to pleasure. I had to stop, I had to walk away from it, to visit the outlines of the pasture and the farm, to carry the glass to the farmhouse so I could know the rooms of its people, to walk again and rest from the persistent unity of the ruin, to lie down in purple vetch and listen to bee-women sip and dangle on the small blossoms. When the sun woke me and I stood up, there was a shape of my own dwelling in the grass.

By now I had a stack of white, six-by-six posts that had held the stanchions in a row, a heap of two-by-fours in random lengths dried hard as iron, twenty-four sheets of tin rusted on the bottom side from generations of cattle-steam and piss in hay, a whole raft of two-by-sixes in twenty-foot lengths, each dried and set precisely to the same roof-sag. When I built my barn, I would turn them over so the roof began with a slight swell. Over time, they would sag back flat and right.

I was just admiring my favorite stick—the four-by-eight haybeam from the gambrel's point, complete with a patch of lichen where it had thrust out into the weather, and a rusted iron ring bolted through that had pulleyed up ton after ton of feed—when a red sports car came creeping along the nail-studded road. I glanced at the clouds reflected in the windshield when it stopped, then lowered the beam to the ground.

The driver waited inside, watching me, or finishing a song on the radio, just long enough to show he was in no hurry, then climbed out slow, slid his hands into his pockets, and looked at the sky.

"Name's Peter. Finding anything good?" He stood by his car. I pointed a crowbar at the haybeam. "Just what you see:

lumber with rot on both ends but some good wood in the middle."

"What about the bees?"

"Right there." I aimed the crowbar at the hive-box humming quietly in the blackberry shade. "I caught all but a few."

"A few?"

"Five."

He nodded slowly, like a bear with ponderous thoughts. "I think I might want those doors," he said, nodding toward the two big wagon doors slapped face-down where they had fallen. He started gingerly around the heap's perimeter in his rubber running shoes. "My wife likes antique stuff—you found anything like that? It doesn't have to be pretty, so long as it's old. My own idea of old is black-and-white TV, but she sees it different."

"There's a wheelbarrow with the bottom rotted out and one handle gone—something like that?"

"She'd love it. Could you wheel it out and leave it by the doors? The County's given me a week to scrape this down to bare dirt. Anything left after Friday will cost me a fine. And the man I hired to take it all down should be along soon. He may have stuff he wants too." He looked at the sky. A quick rain had begun, and he backed away toward the car. "Try to have everything you want out pretty quick. And don't get hurt."

He paused to say more, looked at the ground, then turned and folded himself carefully into the car. The crowbar was warm in my hand, and slick with sweat. The rain felt good. The lights of the car came on, flickered to high-beam, then died as the windshield wipers started to wag. He backed out the long track across the field, his tires spinning a few times on the wet grass.

A cloud moved and sunlight rippled glistening across the field after him. The lumber around me began to steam. My footing was slick but the air was clean. As I worked with steel-hafted hammer in my right hand and crowbar in my left, swinging each long board through the loving rhythm of lift, pound and tease, roll and balance, flip, shove and drop-slap to the stack of clean lumber, I heard the unique machine of the fallen barn flex in the heat, the rippled ping when tin changes its mind, the shriek of a sixteen-penny nail jerked from the sheath rust wedded it to for seventy years, the see-saw rub and grabble of a rafter waggled from the heap, and in a pause the plop of sweat sliding off my elbow to a stone. Before me loomed the raw, steaming tangle of chaos with a history of order, a flavor of tradition, the stiff, wise fiber of old growth; behind me, stacks of lumber rose with a new barn intrinsic in each board, in the rivet of right work I had yet to do to knit it all together again. My hands were twin apprentices to the wreck, to the knowing fragments of joinery still buried there.

As I curled my spine over the tangle to grasp a clear length of one-by-twelve fir, two causes made my task hard: the persistence of the builder, circa 1910, and the haste of the wrecker, 1980. The builder had known how to make things hold, clinching nails that bound the battens down, and pinning the whole fabric of the walls with extra braces scarfed to the frame wherever it might be vulnerable to the wind's pivot or gravity's drag. The wrecker, on the other hand, was in a hurry.

Maybe he heard the bees when he first drove up, and

decided not to go inside at all. Maybe the doors were so woven with thumb-thick ropes of blackberry he didn't take the time to pry them apart and find the mahogany skiff locked together with bronze screws, or the wagon bed, the kerosene lamp, its wick last trimmed before he was born, now crushed flat under a three-hundred pound stick of fir. He never saw the stack of two-by-six spare joists, ten foot long and clear. Those the farmer had set aside for years of so much hay even this cathedral wasn't ample enough. With them he would lay an extra hay-floor over the stanchion alley. Instead, the wrecker threw a grappling hook high over the roof and pulled it all down. That must have brought out the bees to kiss him in the eyes. I found the hook abandoned—it had stabbed into a punky rafter with twenty feet of rope dangling where the wrecker had cut it away and fled. I coiled the rope and hung the hook from a volunteer cherry at the field's edge.

Somewhere way down Boone's Ferry Road I heard the low hum of a big bike coming. I heard it slow for the turn, and accelerate with a roar the last two hundred yards up the side-road toward me. Then it came popping and growling over the field. A nail came out for the crowbar and flipped past my face. I was listening too hard and not watching what I did. I turned.

My face was small and double in the dark glasses on the upturned face of the Gypsy Joker idling his big Harley ten feet away. On the shoulder of his black jacket were stitched the red names of his friends or victims: *Rick, Joe, Rollo*. When the engine rumbled and faded and coughed dead, the black leather of his gloves creaked as he flexed his right hand free.

"Finding some good stuff, buddy?" My double body was still in his glasses. His beard pointed to the field behind me. "I had a nice stack of boards all pulled out over there, but some bastard went and hauled them away."

"Oh, that was me," I said.

"Was, huh?"

"Peter said I get the bees out, I could take any lumber I wanted."

"You talked to Peter about it? I guess that's okay. But what about those bees? Christ, I blow up my truck trying to pull this wreck down, then these bees come busting out with my number in their tails. I don't mess with them little guys. No way." He looked around, raised his hand to his shades, but left them on. "They gone?"

"They're gone," I said.

"Well, hey, soon as I get my truck fixed I'm gonna start hauling this pile to the super dump, so take everything you can." His head turned toward my Chevy low in the grass, then slowly back to me. "I'm on fixed rate. The less I have to haul, the better. Jesus, take it all for firewood. You ain't never going to get another chance like this." He kicked his smoking bike to life with a roar, and had to shout. "I tell you what: I wreck buildings for my living, and I never see pickings easy as these." With a tight nod he turned the bike and bounced across the field, a shrug and hunch restoring his solitude as he waggled away through the grass.

Wind riffled over the mounds and valleys of the blackberry patch, lifting off a harvest of white petals that skimmed across the swell. The two swallows twittered as they spiraled overhead, and a cricket, undisturbed by catastrophe, began to chant from somewhere near the fallen barn doors.

Along toward dusk, as I began sliding the longest boards onto the roof of my car named The Duchess, I saw a little boy come furtively down from the farmhouse, through the lilac hedge, through the wild hawthorn grove and out to the edge of the barn's debris. From the slow bob and swivel of his head, I could read how his gaze followed the outlines of the building that had stood there—first around the footing-wall perimeter, then down the stanchion bay, out into the central floor where the wagon had been, up some invisible ladder to the loft, then south to the back wall. He looked at me. I was part of the treachery. He was polite and said nothing. I began to wrestle a twenty-foot six-by-six, authentic with manure, onto the car.

"It wasn't dangerous," he said quietly, and I knew it was. I got the beam to the balancing joint and stopped to rest.

"Did you go in there a lot?"

"Just sometimes."

"What was it like?"

"It was always dark, and you had to know where you were going. There was broken glass, too, a whole floor of it. But I put a board across it so I could walk."

"What about the ladder?" I said, once I had the beam all the way up at rest on the car roof.

"I knew the good steps to step on. You just go slow, and hold onto other things at the same time. And there were bees in there. They never hurt you. I came up that close." He held his hand in front of his eyes. His face was a blur against the pale swathe of the hawthorn. "They kept working. They never bothered you. Once I even tasted some of their honey that dropped down on the straw." He looked back at me. "What are you going to build here, mister?"

"I'm not going to build anything here," I said, reaching for another board so he wouldn't go away. "Someone just wanted the barn taken down."

"What happened to the bees?"

"They're right there. Can you hear them?" I pointed to the hive-box that glowed a dull white and hummed. We both stood still.

BY DARK I unloaded the mossy timbers and curve-cured boards at my home, carried them one at a time around the house through the memorized tunnel of plum arch, apple tree, grape arbor. I stacked them in different ways, season by season, putting them to bed under tin, listening to the rattle of rain and fitting them in mind on my pillow to an old shape that would happen simply by happening slow. Whenever I hefted a timber so heavy I feared for my collarbone, or teased a splinter from my palm, I remembered how these boards stood face-to-face in a forest harvesting nineteenth-century light, how they slid through the saws side by side, how the green-chain grader's crayon marked them with a C for clear or an S for standard.

Clinched together in the first barn-shape, wood had a memory, and the boards in my yard now curved again for sun and water with a tree's wish, with the honest warp of their character, with history visible in every stress-ripple, every seam of bark or pitch, every conk-wither or knot. The tight grain of slow growth held steady long. But the oldest memory was of earth. Where any board had touched down to the damp floor below architecture, rot took root, branching upward into heart-wood.

I sawed the rot-softened wood away, planed each curve straight, measured the length of firm timber, and began to build the barn again. My industry was slow. The building inspector told me to hurry.

"One hundred and eighty days without visible progress cancels your original permit," he said. "Better get going." But he forgave me. I kept working, resting, remembering the design in the air where the swallows flew. I started remodeling before it was done. The building inspector forgave me even that. Then he retired. His replacement warned me, and then forgave me.

At five a.m., I am in the loft. Dust-colored rafters join in marriage above me. The haybeam behind my head aims toward sunrise. Soon the blackberry pasture out this window will blossom. Soon the bees, daughters of the daughters of the bees I took care of, will winnow out from their white box beyond the pear tree into sunlight.

A NOTE
ON SOURCES

Readers wishing to pursue some of the names and stories in this book will find the following sources helpful:

In the "Introduction," the Kwakiutl names are from Franz Boas, *Geographical Names of the Kwakiutl Indians*, Columbia University Contributions to Anthropology, No. 20 (New York: Columbia University Press, 1934). Thomas Jefferson's word-list is from volume seven of the *Original Journals of the Lewis and Clark Expedition*, 1804–1806, ed. Reuben Gold Thwaites (1905; rpt. New York: Antiquarian Press, 1959). The list of Iroquois lacrosse players is from *Archives: Mirror of Canada Past* (Toronto: University of Toronto Press, 1972).

The literary passages in "Out of This World" are from the standard editions of the authors mentioned.

The Nez Perce Coyote tale in "The Story That Saved Life" is after "Coyote and the Shadow People," in *Coyote Was Going There: Indian Literature of the Oregon Country,* ed. Jarold Ramsey (Seattle: University of Washington Press, 1977). The poem "I Was Old" was written by Vicki Lynne Smith.

References to Ishi in "The Separate Hearth" are from Theodora Kroeber, *Ishi: In Two Worlds* (Berkeley: University of California Press, 1963).

The full story of Grizzly Bear's death in "Dancing Bear of the Siuslaw" is in Leo Frachtenberg, "Siuslawan (Lower Umpqua)," Smithsonian Institution Bureau of American Ethnology, Bulletin 40, Part 2, which forms a part of the *Handbook of American Indian Languages,* ed. Franz Boas (Washington: GPO, 1922).

Some of the stories by old-timers of the Siuslaw Valley in "Dancing Bear of the Siuslaw," "River & Road," and other essays are in the oral history collection of the Siuslaw Pioneer Museum, Florence, Oregon. Thanks to Eileen Huntington, Mary Johnston, Wyma Rogers, and others in Florence for help in collecting these stories, and to the American Revolution Bicentennial Commission of Oregon for supporting the oral history project in 1976.

I would like to thank my agent, Lizzie Grossman, for believing in this book, and to express my gratitude to Gary Luke, Joan Gregory, and my other friends at Sasquatch Books for helping to keep this bundle of stories alive. Their belief in the continuing value of local stories, and their commitment to the cultures of the Pacific Northwest, inspires me. Much has changed in the decade since I first wrote this book, but something wild and original remains—an idea called *hē´ladē,* "having everything right."

Photo by William Stafford

KIM STAFFORD was born in Portland, Oregon, in 1949. Both his father, the poet William Stafford, and his mother, Dorothy, taught, and moved from state to state in search of that ever-elusive better job. They finally returned to Portland, where Stafford spent his youth at the edge of a swathe of Oregon forest somehow left alone in the midst of Portland's growing suburbs. The apprenticeship to that forest was a lasting part of Stafford's childhood: climbing cedar trees, braiding nettle-bark twine, camping in secret places, and imitating his hero, Ishi, the only man of a lost Indian tribe in a favorite childhood book.

Once starting college, Stafford spent twelve years at the University of Oregon before graduating in 1979 with a Ph.D. in medieval literature (after taking courses in architecture, ceramics, photography, cooking, and ethnic dance). Since 1986, Stafford has served as director of the Northwest Writing Institute at Lewis & Clark College in Portland, where he administers an informal and exploratory program for writing in the spirit of ideas. Stafford's work has been widely published, and he is the author of numerous books, including *Wind on the Waves* and *A Gypsy's History of the World*. He lives in Portland with his wife and daughter.